T0368153

THE
CHILL
LAWYER
GUIDE

Cultivating Calm
in the
Legal Profession

ADRIANA M. PARIS

BALBOA.PRESS
A DIVISION OF HAY HOUSE

Balboa Press books may be ordered through booksellers or by contacting:

Balboa Press
A Division of Hay House
1663 Liberty Drive
Bloomington, IN 47403
www.balboapress.com
844-682-1282

Print information available on the last page.

ISBN: 979-8-7652-5607-7 (sc)
ISBN: 979-8-7652-5608-4 (e)

Balboa Press rev. date: 09/25/2024

Contents

Introduction vii

I.   The Essence of Chill 1
     A. What Does It Mean? 1
     B. What Does Chill Look Like in a Lawyer? 23

II. Choosing the Chill Path 37
     A. Chill Body... 38
     B. Chill Mind 42
     C. Chill Spirit.. 51

III. Create Your Chill 61
     A. Choosing Your Career Vision.............................. 61
     B. Building a Life Around the Vision....................... 84
     C. Executing on Your Vision 105

Final Word 115
Endnotes 117

Introduction

I wrote my first book *Rising Lawyer: from Summer Associate to First-Year Associate*[1] as a guidebook for those entering the legal profession based on my experiences as a lawyer. When deciding on a topic for your first book, the general advice is "Write what you know." So I put together a first-hand encounter of what I had seen and what I had experienced so far in the legal profession. It was truly a passion project to type the words that I wished I had read when I was a law student interviewing for the first time or during my first week on the job as an associate attorney. It was almost surreal to then see those words printed inside of a book that I could share with anyone in law school or preparing for law school. Following the publication of *Rising Lawyer,* I began to get questions from more seasoned attorneys about whether there was anything in that book that would be useful to them—the implied assumption being that they were well past law school and needed more grown up advice. It was during that time that I heard someone on a podcast say that she taught to others the lessons that she needed to learn herself. A lightbulb went off: what was the lesson I still needed to learn after a decade of practicing law? And more importantly, what did my lawyer friends need to learn?

So I decided to write this book for a specific type of lawyer I've encountered again and again throughout my career: the insecure overachiever. You know the one—type A personality, people-pleaser, teacher's pet, gets good grades, always goes for the extra credit, chases prestige, and yet still doesn't believe she's good enough. Maybe that's you. Maybe that's a partner with whom you work. It was certainly me. I first learned about this term through a conversation with some lawyer co-workers—all women—who expressed just how much they identified with that description. They told me how they always went above and beyond, even as children, even on seemingly insignificant tasks, because they simply felt like doing an okay job wasn't an option. They sought approval from their parents, then teachers, then professors, now bosses. They continually chased the next level in their careers despite being unable to articulate *why* they actually wanted that promotion. Still, the more they worked (oftentimes for very little actual praise), the more unworthy they felt.

The hamster wheel of . . .

hard work → accomplishment →

temporary dopamine hit from positive
feedback → start all over again

. . . is exhausting and eventually leads to burnout

Unsurprisingly, insecure overachievers end up in the legal field where the main currency is people-pleasing (or client service as we affectionately call it). These types make the perfect law firm associates because no amount of work can break them if it is all in the name of excellent legal service and the promise of promotion to this vague title called "Partner." Being a lawyer might seem like a niche profession (and in many aspects, it's certainly an exclusionary one), but according to the latest American Bar Association (ABA) survey, there are more than 1.3 million lawyers in the United States.[2] While of course not all 1.3 million legal professionals have the same personality traits, if you're a lawyer, you are well-aware of the groupthink that has developed in our profession: work more, do more, strive for more, and do it again the next day and the next day.

The byproduct of these tendencies shows up in the form of

harrowing statistics for the lawyer cohort. ABA's monumental 2017 National Task Force on Lawyer Well-Being unveiled the following numbers from 13,000 lawyers surveyed:

- 21 to 36% of the respondents qualified as problem drinkers

- 28% suffered from depression

- 19% suffered from anxiety

- 23% experienced stress[3]

In 2023, the American Lawyer and Law.com conducted a survey of 3,000 lawyers and reported the following:

- 38.27% of the participants felt depressed

- A whopping 71.10% suffered from anxiety

- 50.93% feel a sense of failure and self-doubt

- 26.33% have increased their use of drugs and/or alcohol as a result of their work environment[4]

We have become numb to these statistics. Worse, we have normalized them. None of us wants these numbers to be true; yet, we don't feel like we have any control over the nature of practicing law in its current state. We accept the stress, the depression, the anxiety, the substance abuse, the numbing, the suicidal thoughts (and increasingly, the deaths by suicide) as if they are non-negotiables. We all want better, but this problem seems so much bigger than us that we just fold and give up. Generations punt the problem to the next one: millennials were supposed to fix this (we haven't), maybe Gen Z will get it right (maybe, but why don't we help?), and so on. And the numbers only get worse. Do we actually believe that the state of the profession will improve in the next 10 or 20 years?

Many lawyers I've spoken to simply don't know how to live another way. Their fear of "letting the foot off the gas" reigns so supreme that they would rather forego time with family, health, hobbies, and friendships than risk being seen as a subpar performer. When I ask them if they believe that giving 80% effort is still significantly better than average, I am met with confused looks quickly followed by a dismissive wave, as if they are truly incapable of doing less than 100%. But all of us—from junior associates to partners to law firm owners—need to take a step back and evaluate why we are doing what we do, how we can improve or rescript our work to fit our life goals, and how we can actually get to a place where we enjoy our careers. As bestselling author and productivity guru Greg McKeown wrote in a June 2023 article, "The 85% rule counterintuitively suggests that to reach maximum output, you need to refrain from giving maximum effort. Operating at 100% effort all of the time will result in burnout and ultimately less-optimal results."[5] He offered the example of Olympic runners who end up running a slower race overall when they are told to reach their maximum effort too soon. Optimized effort holds up much better than continuous 100% effort in the long run. The old adage then remains true: our careers are a marathon, not a sprint. So why are we running at 100 miles an hour 24/7?

The 2020-2023ish pandemic made these insecure overachievers burn out at a rate that alarmed not just them, but those around them. Always the top performers and go-to lawyers at their firms, these individuals finally crashed and burned, much to the shock of their peers and bosses. If law firms can't count on their lawyers to bill, bill, bill during times of great stress, how can they continue bringing in massive profits? If Jane, the highest performing associate, can no longer keep her shit together because her spouse has been fired and her best friend has long COVID and her neighbor is battling cancer, then what can be expected of underperforming associates? If Julian, the firm's best business development lawyer, needs to sign off at 4:00 pm every weekday to spend time with his autistic child because his partner's new job doesn't allow him this time off, then

x

how can the firm depend on junior associates who refuse to go into the office to pick up the business development slack? All the while, law firms go on as they always have, churning off massive profits year after year and offering their associates office yoga and Zoom cooking classes as small indulgences for all the hard work.

This is where this book comes in. Look, the legal profession will take everything it can from us, greedy for our attention and insatiable for our devotion. The law is not a person: it will not apologize for the many inconveniences it brings into our lives nor will it reward us for the endless number of ours we put into perfecting our craft. The truth is that no one is coming to save us. It is entirely up to us as individuals to create the life we want, to put up our own boundaries, and to design a life worth living. There are many lawyers who are content in their careers and who may be saying "It could be a lot worse." Yes, but it could also be a lot better. The delta between a misery and happiness at work is huge. Why would we only shoot for the middle ground?

What has been guiding me all these years is the profound realization that how we spend our days is how we spend our years. Life isn't made up of two or three huge, course-altering inflection points where we have to make THE big decision; rather, it's made up of small junctures, most of which pass us by without fanfare, where we choose how we want to live daily. This book is a compilation of the seemingly trivial decisions we make and how they impact our overall wellbeing as lawyers. As I often say, small wins carry the day. Once we become more intentional about how spend our minutes and hours, we will slowly start to build the quilt of our lives, the pattern that creates our legacy.

Join me as we will discover together the possibilities of making for ourselves a fulfilled, balanced, and healthy life.

I

The Essence of Chill

A. What Does It Mean?

In the Beginning

My first glimpse of chill began, funny enough, in law school. As an immigrant without any adults in my family who had experienced American higher education, let alone anyone who had gone to law school, I was blissfully unaware of all the mental drama associated with obtaining a legal education. I didn't know what rankings meant, or the importance of on-campus interviews, or the Socratic method, the difference between grading on or writing on a journal and why the hell would anyone even volunteer for this extracurricular, or why law schools spend so much time on legal theory and such little time on legal practice—a fact which I still don't understand after over a decade practicing law. I entered law school with the optimism of a Golden Retriever. I was quite literally just happy to be there. I went to class with the sole purpose of absorbing information. I made friends because they were fun and interesting people, not because I believed they had something to offer me. I talked to professors and deans and career services professionals to gain insight into their chosen professions and the knowledge they had gathered along the way. I had fun. I went to football games. I spent weekends getting to know my new city and its surrounding areas. I went to all the local restaurants, even on an extremely frugal budget. I made friends from other programs, like our university's medical pharmacy schools. I enjoyed law school tremendously.

Looking back, I believe there is something profoundly freeing about not over-analyzing every aspect of a situation. Entering a new experience without having researched the ins and outs of what you might or might not find, putting your expectations aside and just taking yourself along for the ride are simply not within our practice today. But my 20-something-year-old brain was onto something. Without realizing it at the time, I essentially developed a sense of surrender to the experience of law school. I saw that the entire institution was much larger than me and that I could not change the many, many years upon which it had been created, so I allowed myself to receive all the wisdom, the hard lessons, the good and the bad without judging my value as a law student or future lawyer. In ancient yoga teachings, there is something called "aparigraha," loosely translated as non-possessiveness or non-attachment. It is one of the Yamas in the Eight Limbs of Yoga and it teaches practitioners to take only what we need, keep only what serves us in the moment, and to let go when the time is right. In the sacred text Bhagavad Gita, Lord Krishna says: "Let your concern be with action alone, and never with the fruits of action. Do not let the results of action be your motive, and do not be attached to inaction."[6] While many interpret this teaching to encourage disposal of physical belongings, aren't there mental belongings we can get rid of as well?

My law school was a true teacher and I was an unselective student. Don't get me wrong, I wasn't just floating around aimlessly: I had a goal to do well enough to get a job after graduation. I was certainly dedicated to that goal and I served it by being studious and conscientious. But I also experimented with taking whatever classes interested me, joining groups that seemed fun even if they weren't necessarily resume boosts, and not trying to fit in whatever ideal mold law schools project onto their students. Aspiring law students are often advised to treat law school like a job, and I believe the better advice is to give it the same *time commitment* as you would a full-time job. But remember that you're paying for this degree, not the other way around. Also, don't take it so seriously. It's such a fleeting time in your overall life trajectory and it can bring so many new experiences, ideas, and lifelong friends if you allow it.

Although I had an extraordinarily positive law school experience, I do have one regret and that is that I didn't stop to ask myself what exactly I wanted to do after law school, and most importantly, why. Even though I acknowledged that I didn't have any preconceived ideas about law school or legal practice before arriving here, I really should have taken the time to gather more information once I was in the throes of on-campus interviews. I should have assessed my strengths, my not-so-strengths, my interests, what I could live with in a career and what would be a bottom-line violation (to quote attorney Michael F. Melcher's excellent read *The Creative Lawyer*). The only question I asked myself was whether I wanted to be a litigator or a transactional lawyer. That seemed to be the only inquiry other law students were undertaking, so I just followed suit. During interviews, I basically accepted the highest-paying job I was offered, which coincidentally also employed some of the nicest lawyers I had met and called it a decision. But it wasn't really a decision—it was the default state.

You're not making a decision if you only see one option.

Humans are hardwired to choose the default choice, the status quo, the safest and most obvious action. It's partly because we are so afraid of failing and partly because having to assess multiple possibilities is exhausting. We don't do a good enough job at engaging in deep thought or metacognition, where we actively evaluate our own patterns of decision-making and reflect on how we view the world and why. Instead we take the most direct route to where we think we want to go and call it a decision. Both the route itself and the destination might be unsuitable for us, but we often don't realize it until we've already packed our bags, started driving, and are nearing our journey's end. There's a quote often attributed to Chinese philosopher Lao Tzu that goes like: "If you do not change direction, you may end up where you are heading." In other words, blindly following the path laid out ahead of you will lead you exactly in that direction regardless of whether you intended to end up there.

So too I followed the path of least resistance—litigation— mainly because it seemed more "fun" than transactional law and because people told me that I would get to do more writing as a litigator. What I didn't realize was that "fun" is seldom associated with high-stakes civil litigation and that my writing would be largely template-based and dictated by others. Had I taken the necessary time for introspection, I would have learned that one of my top values is authenticity and that being constrained in the way I communicate (verbally or through writing) is soul-sucking to me. I also would have learned that I operate in the gray much better than in black and white. Despite the ongoing joke that the only legally correct answer is "it depends," the legal profession remains largely seeded in right or wrong, yes or no, this applicable precedent or a de novo analysis. Lawyers like knowing *the one* answer, the clear way forward, the proven way to resolve an issue. Meanwhile, I love thinking creatively and considering multiple possibilities regardless of how it's been done in the past. This aspect of my personality wasn't necessarily a hindrance in my chosen profession, but I would be lying if I said it was celebrated.

And, this might shock my legal colleagues and former law firm bosses, but I am not the most detail-oriented person. Mic drop, I know. The average person would consider me extremely meticulous, but on the legal scale of negligence to perfectionism, I fall somewhere in the middle. It's not that I am unable to focus on the details; instead, I find much more joy in thinking through high-level strategy and creating big picture solutions rather than tracking every comma. I am more energized by putting together an outline for a motion than I am proofreading the final product. As an associate, I loathed the constant revising and perfecting of every single draft before filing with the court; I often deviously fantasized e-filing the first draft with only spellcheck as my editor.[7] If I had given this career more thought while in law school, I also would have likely began developing the chill lawyer identity that took me years to understand and appreciate. The long hours spent at the office + the weekend work I constantly needed to catch up on + the numerous trials involved in a litigation practice at a big law firm were never compatible with my personality or my values. But I didn't know what I didn't ask myself.

> Sometimes the hardest thing to learn is the least complicated one, like what you like and what you don't like.

Despite lacking awareness over what I wanted in a career, I did begin a gratitude practice while in law school. It started as a night-time ritual before drifting off to sleep where I would take a minute to thank my lucky stars for allowing me the opportunity to study at the best law school in Florida, surrounded by such brilliant colleagues and professors. The level of instruction and the substance of the material were such a step up from my relatively unchallenging undergraduate courses that I felt both underqualified and energized to be here. So every night I would do a quick scan of how my day had gone and would send gratitude to whoever is up there for giving me another day to expand my knowledge. I don't think I necessarily appreciated the benefits while in law school, but over time, they became abundantly obvious: enumerating all the reasons you have to be thankful eventually reduces the number of things you *think* you need to be happy. Many of us intrinsically understand that only a few items bring us true contentment—family, health, a purpose in life, some financial resources, physical safety—yet we all get caught up in a hedonistic wheel of yearning for more and comparing our haves to other people's. The problem is that we keep moving the goal posts farther away each time we "achieve" something we thought we wanted, the satisfaction lasts for a couple of days at most, then we are back on the hamster wheel chasing after the next thing. It's not until you learn to truly appreciate what you have and feel in your heart that it's *enough* that you can be released from the trap.

I wrote in my last book that I believe having a gratitude practice can also teach you to listen to your inner voice and in turn, develop your intuition. That's because it helps build the quiet muscle. Most of us live our lives reacting to everything and everyone around us. It's not entirely our fault—tech companies have spent millions and millions of dollars researching and perfecting ways to steal our attention and constantly grab our focus. We've become addicted to the rollercoaster of high jitters of social media notifications when we feel anxious and the low lull of mindless scrolling when we feel bored. We don't know how to self-soothe, self-entertain, self-motivate. I wish I could give you Buzzfeed-type list of three ways to detach from your devices and quickly achieve inner peace, but that doesn't exist. Rather, I invite you to start with a daily or nightly gratitude practice, which eventually you can turn into an opportunity for solitude and listening to your own thoughts. What do you want to tell yourself? How do you want to interact with your inner teacher? How can you turn down the volume on the outside world and turn it up within yourself?

Law school was also my first true interaction with people's competitiveness. Now, I didn't grow up in some idyllic commune where everyone worked toward a common resource and no one competed for anything, but I think by nature, I am just not someone who is competitive. Even when I played team sports growing up, I never really compared myself with other players. I was happy when our team won, of course, but I wasn't despondent when we lost. I am my own biggest competition and worst critic. I truly don't believe that my only chance at success comes at someone else's failure. We can all be successful. Well, except that is quite literally false in most law schools where students are graded on a curve. If I get an A on a final exam, someone must get a C. Law schools award the highest grade in each class, the best mock argument, the top journal submission, etc. Individual performance is evaluated based on how much "better" it is than someone else's performance. And yet, from my experience as a practicing attorney, there isn't much that differentiates the C-students from the A-students.

Even as we all left law school behind and progressed in our careers, it appears that many lawyers still behaved as if they were graded on an imaginary curve where one's performance could only be deemed A-worthy if someone else's was a D. I observed this in big law firms, small shops, in house, you name it. This internal urge to constantly compare oneself to others and decide at every turn "I am better than Nelly, but not as good as Thomas, therefore my value as a person lies somewhere in the middle of the curve" is all-prevailing within the legal profession. It plagues new lawyers, seasoned lawyers, lawyers who come from a long line of other lawyers, first-generation lawyers, lawyers with student loans, and wealthy lawyers all alike. It's as if we all signed an imaginary oath upon graduating law school to continue this inherent competition with each other until we die. It would be too easy to say law school is to blame for this and so law schools need to change. Now, I do believe that law schools *do* play a role in harnessing this mode of behavior, but at the end of the day, we are fully formed, independent adults who have agency over how we think and how we act.

Right? You feel like you have agency over your own thoughts, don't you? When you tell yourself that you're not smart enough or prepared enough or that surely you must have missed something in the sixth draft of that motion? Or when you don't speak up during a meeting because the more senior lawyers in the room must know better and your contribution would be stupid anyway? Or when you don't apply for that dream job because it requires five years of law firm experience and you only have four years and three months? When you make a tiny mistake in an email, then spend the rest of the day (and night) beating yourself up over it? When you're overwhelmed but continue taking on assignments because being a lawyer should be hard and miserable, right? We have so many negative thoughts running through our minds, constantly telling us we're not good enough and by extension, that someone else is better than us, and yet we have accomplished so much. We finished law school and we passed the bar exam, gosh darn it. Why do we torture ourselves with such hurtful thoughts?

In the words of philosopher John Locke:

What worries you, masters you.

Our thoughts—conscious or unconscious, positive, or damaging—become our actions and how we carry ourselves in the world. Learning how to separate our thoughts from facts and to quit assigning them an emotional value is a lifelong practice. This book alone won't have all the answers. But I will tell you exactly how I was able to overcome years of self-imposed perfectionism and intrusive thoughts, which then allowed me to live a happier, freer, more impactful life. You might be thinking, "Wait a minute, Adriana, I thought you said that you were super chill in law school!" Well, I was. I was chill all the way until something cracked me in my fourth year of practice.

My Period of No Chill, or How I Survived a Horrible Boss

In many ways I lucked out with my first job out of law school. My haphazard job search led me to a big law firm with a smaller satellite office in Tampa, Florida. So while I technically worked for a large law firm with hundreds of lawyers scattered around the country, my own little world comprised of ten or so lawyers who took me under their wings and mentored the hell out of me. I eventually got to work with lawyers and staff in several of our firm's offices, but I truly learned everything I know about civil litigation from those ten folks. If you were to find me in my first, second or third of practice and ask me how I felt, I would've said "Great!" I legitimately had very few complaints. I worked hard and the work itself wasn't thrilling, but I had no other responsibilities and, more importantly, nothing else to compare it to. This was my first official grown-up office job and I simply didn't have any expectations. Are you sensing a theme yet?

Soon after I started, I developed a reputation as the dependable associate, always willing to take on more projects and turn around assignments in record time. While speed-reading and analysis have always been my superpowers, it was the anxiety of having a much-too-long to-do list that fueled my quick work. I wasn't particularly organized or methodical in how I approached these assignments; I just basically did them as fast as I could so I could move on to the next. Was I the most detail-oriented? No. Did my research encompass every nuanced issue? Nope. But I kept getting more and more work, as the old saying goes: "Law practice is a cake-eating contest where the prize is more cake." One year, I went to three trials, each lasting several weeks. I literally never said no and everyone I worked with loved this about me. At one of my yearly evaluations, a partner said that I was a smiling energizer bunny. Thanks, I guess. Last minute jury research? Adriana will do it. Random six-hour trip with an expert witness to an independent medical examination? Adriana will go. Fly to rural Oklahoma to find a witness who's hiding from us? Adriana will meet you there. Internal memo on a business issue that will never actually be read? Hopping on Westlaw right now. You can probably guess where this work ethic landed me: straight to burnout-ville.

As I was nearing my fourth year of practice, I finally lifted my head and looked around me for the first time. I mean, *really* looked around me. Most of the lawyers in my office were homegrown, meaning that they had started working at the firm out of law school, and they had essentially never left. They seemed happy, I guess. But not really excited or fulfilled. They drudged on and on every day, cogs in a massive litigation wheel over which they had little control, and which didn't appear to bring about any real satisfaction. They were well-paid, of course. But every day looked predictably the same. All of this might sound fine to you and it may very well have been fine for them, but I eventually began itching for more. I don't consider myself a risk taker, but I do have a tendency to obsess about future me. Where will I be in five years? Do I want to stay at this job, lulled into the same sense of security that my colleagues seem to have attained? Do I want to be working on the same case in which I served initial discovery five years ago and which still hasn't gone to trial? Do I want to interact with the same clients, same expert witnesses, same legal issues over and over again? Will future me be happy at this firm in five years? More importantly, what kind of life did I owe future me?

The answer, loud and clear, was that I didn't want my career
to just *happen* to me while I idly stood by and watched.
I wanted to be an active participant, not a spectator.

I didn't know exactly what I wanted to do, but I was pretty sure I didn't want to work for another law firm, so I took the second option that came to mind: an in-house role. Nowadays it's quite common for a junior attorney to get an in-house job but several years ago, it was not. Not only that, there weren't a lot of in-house positions posted in Florida. But I found one! I was hired as a Director of Litigation, the youngest director by far within the company, and for a position I most certainly wasn't qualified. Looking back now, I have to say I admire my unbridled confidence. I shouldn't have even applied for this job, let alone make it through four rounds of interviews and on top of it, negotiate a higher salary for myself. Past me was a badass. As a side note, *everyone* has moments where one has acted in such a bold and powerful way that almost surprises the present self; yes, even you have them. I strongly suggest you make it a practice to collect all of these instances so that you can reflect on your own victories when you're feeling down. I have found it to be the most effective way to combat impostor syndrome.

Back to my new and wholly undeserved job as a director. I wasn't nervous about my abilities to learn the job and use my almost four years of litigation in a way that would serve the company, but I did not realize how difficult my working relationship with my new boss would be. As someone who is generally easygoing and has had tremendous practice navigating social interactions as an immigrant, I never expected to be placed in a situation where I simply did not know how to interact with this individual in a way that didn't take my anxiety to unparalleled levels. This is what broke me.

Let me be clear: this chapter isn't about badmouthing another lawyer or my chance at a juicy "tell-all." This is more about reckoning with myself about how I handled a difficult circumstance to the best of my ability and how I came out on the other side with a completely new perspective. I hope that if you find yourself in a tough spot, remember that sometimes storms clear your path instead of disrupting it. Every challenge is·an opportunity for building resilience so that one day, when you have overcome this obstacle, you can look back and feel gratitude for the growth it provided you. It's so hard to see the other side when you're smack in the thick of it, but truly, things do get better. I am writing this chapter as much for myself as I am for you, reader, because I know that I will again encounter hard situations and I hope I will meet them with grace and a little wisdom.

So what went so horribly wrong in my new job? Honestly, it's hard to tell. While I worked there and in the years since I left that role, I spoke with others who reported to my boss and even a few folks who didn't, and they all had similarly awful interactions with him. In my particular situation, I believe it was a perfect storm of: bad temper + micromanagement + lack of trust + possibly some weird fear that I wanted to take his job. I can't say that we had a honeymoon period where he was kind to me. From the beginning, there seemed to be an unpredictability as to how he would respond to what I said or did—he would either support me and agree with my decision or completely lose his mind over how I could possibly be so stupid as to say or do what I did. I truly never knew what mood he would be in and thus quickly began to second-guess everything I did. This self-doubt seeped into everything from planning a team member's birthday to seemingly innocuous internal emails to settlement negotiations. His anger didn't discriminate between things that truly wouldn't matter the next day or actions that could legally bind the company. Strangely enough, he usually worked himself up much more with the former than the latter. He was a screamer, my boss. I don't mean to say that he raised his voice when he was upset; I am talking about screaming and shouting and cursing while he was angry. He did it to me, he did it to employees who didn't even report to him, and he sometimes did it to his same-level colleagues. It was such blind rage that I don't think anyone knew how to respond to it, so we mostly just stood there, looking at the wall, waiting for the tantrum to stop.

There were so many instances that would fill up an entire novel, but two really stick in my mind as turning points in my personal and professional growth. The first occurred when he asked me to help him turn around a team member whom he claimed was not performing well. Even though I was a director at this company, I had no direct reports as my boss insisted I learn his management style first.[8] When he asked me to help with this particular employee, what he really wanted was someone to fix a "problem" that he wasn't emotionally equipped to handle. This employee really didn't have a performance issue; he—like all of us in that department—had a boss issue. The employee was unmotivated, anxious, and seriously questioning his judgment, all because our boss constantly put him down. He had reached his breaking point. I knew this was a losing assignment for me: I could never instill sufficient confidence in this employee to turn around his performance; at best, I could empathize with him and gently suggest that he look for another job. I tried both approaches without much success. My boss was only temporarily pleased as he avoided having a tough conversation with the employee, but eventually became irate as no "progress" was being made. In the end, he just found the answer he wanted to find: that I wasn't ready to be a people manager.

The employee eventually left. Of course he did. I should have left then too, but I was too stubborn to admit defeat. I envisioned my boss smugly walking around the office announcing that I couldn't cut it in-house, that I was too inexperienced, too soft. I didn't want to give him that satisfaction so instead I stayed and continued being miserable, which ironically also gave him satisfaction. Here might be the biggest lesson I have learned and if it helps anyone just a smidge, I can go to heaven happy:

Until you value yourself, no one else will.

What point was I proving by staying in this job? I didn't earn my boss's respect or kindness or even general concern. When a hurricane hit Florida, leaving many of us without power, he never once inquired how we all fared or if our homes suffered damage; instead, he told us we should go into the office because it still had power and air conditioning (a not-so-subtle hint to just get back to work and shut up). He didn't care about our families or pets or general well-being, despite the fact that he boasted often about his overachieving kids and his beautiful house on the water. Do you know how awkward it is to listen to someone's lengthy personal stories, knowing that you can't share your own? Or that if you do share something, it will be twisted into a negative? One week I had to leave the office early two days in a row to take care of something at home and told him so in advance, knowing that he watched the hallways like a hawk to see when his team came and went. His response: "You're aware that this isn't a part-time job?"

What ultimately convinced me that I was fighting a losing battle, a battle that I realized I didn't want to win even if it were possible, was when my boss asked me to postpone an already-booked vacation to Europe because a project that had gone on for several months would not be completed by the time I left. Now, this wasn't a project that I even played a significant part in, or something that had come up unexpectedly, or one where we would have deadlines during my trip. No, this was an ongoing project that began long before my trip and that would continue after my return. I was only going to be gone for a week. Not only did he ask me to cancel this trip as indifferently if it were a dentist appointment, he actually got irritated at my initial defiance. How dare I say no to him? I was on the verge of tears trying to explain that my husband and I had booked our flights and hotels and that he had already taken off work for this trip. When he said that I would have to cancel and that was the end of the discussion, I walked back to my desk shaking. I felt both weak for my inability to stand up to him and stupid for thinking I ever had a chance.

After returning from my postponed trip, I gave my two-week notice. He wasn't upset or surprised or anything, really. Over my last two weeks, he obsessed over ensuring that I had transferred everything over to outside counsel and addressed every outstanding issue I had. On my last day, shortly after lunch, he came to my desk and told me that I didn't need to aimlessly wait around until the end of the day, and I could leave whenever I wanted. What a heartfelt goodbye! I am pretty sure I floated out of that building. I have never seen him or spoken to him since that day and I hope I never do.

If I am being completely honest with myself and with you, dear reader, I have carried around a lot of shame over how this experience played out. For many years, I blamed myself for being weak and unable to outsmart this man. I kept replaying certain interactions in my head and revising them with me standing up for myself and my coworkers, and eloquently telling him to buzz off. I just tortured myself though because I couldn't go back and act differently. Slowly I learned to empathize with past me because she was doing her best given the tools she had as a fourth-year lawyer. How I want to end this chapter is by reaffirming that two things can be true at the same time: yes, I had a lot to learn a lot in this role, and yes, I should have nonetheless been treated with respect and offered constructive feedback rather than constant scolding. It has taken me many years to believe both parts of this story.

Finding My Chill

I don't wish this experience on anyone and some days I can hardly believe I endured it myself. But I cannot stress how formative it was for me as a lawyer and as a person. Subconsciously I made myself certain promises that I still keep to this day, like always put myself first, follow my inner wisdom, don't compromise my integrity or confidence, and don't allow mean bosses to tell me what to do. Consciously I developed a motto that I live by today: the chill lawyer. I resolved that I would always protect my emotional, physical, and mental well-being above all else. I knew that this new lifestyle would require some hard boundaries, as well as learning to detach my self-worth from society's expectations of a typical lawyer. I would also have to let go of the busyness badge that is so beloved by our legal profession. But this new maxim would be worth it because I could maintain it for the rest of my life. The chill lawyer encompasses five areas:

Confidence

Health

Intuition

Learning, and

Light

After this ill-fated in-house experience, I returned to my old firm with a new attitude. It's tough to even admit this but I was so scarred from this job that I couldn't accept other in-house positions. Isn't it funny how our brains are so wired to protect us that they will go to extreme lengths to rationalize irrational fears? Obviously not all in-house lawyers would be as awful as my former boss; logically, I understood this and yet I couldn't shake off the anxious thoughts swirling around my head that I would be repeating this disaster all over again. I remember leaving an interview for an in-house counsel role with a large hospital and just trying to find clues about my would-be boss's hidden cruelty or terrible management style. Even when I couldn't find any and even after completing my second round of interviews with my would-be colleagues, I just couldn't commit to working there. Hindsight being 20-20, that job would have been perfectly fine, although I believe I still would have eventually left the practice of law.

After my crappy in-house experience, I also felt the need to be safe, to be surrounded by lawyers who knew me and trusted me, and didn't scream profanities weekly. Career experts suggest that every new job be accompanied by both a salary increase and a title promotion. That is great advice if you're lucky enough to leave a job unscathed, but it doesn't work when you are figuratively wounded. Sometimes a career climb feels too difficult and instead, we do a lateral crab walk to the next best opportunity. If you are also facing a similar decision, I urge you to remember that the choice of an upward move is not always black and white, and sometimes our individual circumstances require us to choose jobs in the gray.

Returning to my first job offered the perfect opportunity for me to practice my new chill motto. I first had to work on getting my confidence back. Those who know me personally are probably shocked to hear that my confidence took a hit during my in-house stint because I always *appear* self-assured. But this is the plague of insecure overachievers, isn't it? We seem to have it all together, juggling priorities like Cirque du Soleil® pros, smiling the entire time, never afraid to drop the ball. The façade works for a while—sometimes for years—until it becomes increasingly more challenging to keep it up. Learning to trust myself and to actually feel confident was a process but working alongside my friends again was immensely helpful.

I also gave myself some grace by choosing an alternative work schedule with a lower billable hourly requirement. Part of my decision was due to sheer burnout and part of it was because I knew I wanted to rebuild my caseload slowly and still have time for my health, travel (on my own schedule, not someone else's), and my new puppy, Cooper. It wasn't an easy decision to make. I took a pay cut and was no longer on partnership track. But it was a confident decision because it gave me the most precious resource: time, more specifically command over my own time. With a reduced workload, I was able to regain mastery of my professional skills in my own time and reestablish the belief that I was smart and competent. As a result, my work flourished, and not only did I consistently receive praise, I also *felt* good about my work in a way that I hadn't when I worked in-house. I also got opportunities that were above my "level" because I was truly exceeding expectations. Partners from other offices started requesting to work with me. The lesson from all of this was plain:

So often we achieve more by doing less.

But it wasn't all rainbows and roses. My old habits started creeping back up and I frequently had to stop myself from taking yet another assignment and yet another "super quick project that shouldn't take more than an hour" (spoiler alert: they *always* take more than an hour!). Even though I was way less stressed and my body no longer tensed whenever I received an email or I was called into someone's office, I knew that I had to stay on top of regulating my workflow because no one else would do it for me. If I repeated my old pattern of always saying yes, my reward would simply be more work. I also had to learn to listen to myself: if my initial reaction to a new project was a loud no, then I needed to honor that instead of forcing myself to push through in order to get to a yes. Every time you choose to do something, you're by default not choosing another thing or several other things. Everything in life is a tradeoff and it's up to us individually to decide what we want and what we don't want.

I also took this time to work on my second and possibly the most important piece of my chill lawyer motto: health. There are many facets of health and I will discuss them more in depth in the next chapter, but I personally focused on quality sleep and exercise during this time. As the years went on and I added other layers to my routine, I still believe that sleep is the most important. I know, who wants to read about sleep? If you're a lawyer, I want you to think about sleep as a court-imposed deadline that you must meet daily. Sure, you can negotiate an extension from time to time, but the only party who benefits from an extension is usually the one who would be better off not getting it. In other words, getting quality sleep is the equivalent of doing your due diligence as a lawyer to move a case along. You can't put it off, you can't assign it to someone else, you can't take shortcuts. You might get away with skirting your duties every once in a while, but you better not make it a habit.

Now I will admit that throughout my life, I've been pretty good at both exercising and getting sufficient sleep. The latter is actually an ongoing joke with my friends and family, so much so that my maid of honor mentioned during her speech at my wedding that she doesn't expect me to answer the phone after 8:00 pm because I'm in bed. It's true—I basically have the bedtime of a toddler. I've also been an athlete growing up and, as such I've always kept an exercise routine, even through law school and weeks-long trials. But even the habits that come to you naturally can fall by the wayside when your body is feeling the constant pressure of stress. So even though I went through the motions of exercising and getting to bed early, I really was just going through the motions without paying attention to how I felt. And then I got injured. Not in an acute, torn ACL or pulled hamstring way, but in a more subtle and chronic way. My muscles began aching, sometimes after a workout, but frequently just as I would be sitting in my car driving to work or walking down the hallways in my office. I felt it mostly in my hips, shoulders, and the sides of my neck. It was like a dull tension that would be slightly alleviated with stretching and yoga but would inevitably return a couple of days later.

I did what any normal person with health insurance does in this country and saw a plethora of health professionals and medical doctors. I got X-rays and CT scans and chiropractic care and sports massages. Everything worked temporarily but nothing lasted. I defeatedly resigned myself to the thought that maybe I was just getting older? But then I talked to friends who were the same age as me, who had jobs they liked, who had hobbies and passions, who took personal time off just because, and who were not experiencing the type of pain I was. Spoiler alert: these friends were not lawyers.[9] What started out as a genuine effort to get my body back in check became a deeper dive into somatic symptoms of stress, where seemingly physical aches or digestive issues are actually caused by anxiety, depression, and other neurological conditions. Since then I've read and heard numerous stories of body pains and illnesses disappearing after a person changes his or her life circumstances, whether a career change or a divorce or a move to another country. This was another sign that I needed to fiercely protect my newly embraced chill life. If I didn't, I would easily slip back into my old ways of practicing law and my body was sending me SOS signals to avoid that.

This is also where my intuition came in. After 30-plus years on this Earth listening to what other people thought I should do or who I should be or how I should show up as a person, learning to listen to myself was akin to learning a new language but without any dictionary. In her brilliant book *Playing Big*, women's leadership expert Tara Mohr refers to our inner mentor as the voice inside each of us who knows what we need deep down and how to get there. Juxtaposing the inner mentor with the inner critic we're all too familiar with, she writes: "The inner critic demands our attention. The inner mentor waits to be paid attention to. Where the inner critic rants and raves, the inner mentor speaks softly. The inner critic interrupts and invades our thinking. The inner mentor almost always waits to be asked for input before she speaks."[10]

That last line is critical—our intuition doesn't just pop out of nowhere waving a big yellow flag, screaming "Do this now!" Rather, it's a slowly developing muscle. We need to get quiet and remove all outside noise in order to really hear ourselves. But once that voice starts speaking and we allow it to show us our next steps, it will never stop guiding us. The reason why it is so important to let that inner voice speak is because otherwise, we will just continue stumbling through life, following someone's else path or someone else's dream.

If you don't know where you're going, how will you get there?

One thing I did as soon as I returned to my first job was to sit down and create a list of work I enjoyed doing, work I disliked doing, and work I could tolerate every so often. I unimaginatively called it my "Likes/dislikes/tolerates" list and I still recommend this list to anyone who will listen, lawyer or not. It was a tedious process. I made myself list out every granular, mundane, simple task I ever did and assign it inside one of the three buckets. To my surprise, the list of work I enjoyed and the list of assignments I hated were nearly the same length. The tasks I could tolerate were numerous and varying in degrees of substance: from creating PowerPoint presentations to writing legal articles to helping other lawyers with their time entries.[11] Some of the items I included were truly one-off projects that I wouldn't be expected to do repeatedly, but I wanted this list to be all-encompassing. I am not exaggerating when I say that writing out this list was life-changing. Seeing my likes and dislikes written one by one on paper brought me such clarity and helped me see patterns I had never contemplated before. There were several observations I made:

• I often reject the status quo and having to follow a process just because "it's always been done this way" really grinds my gears.

• I have a slight authority problem. I don't totally disrespect authority figures (I am still a lawyer!), but I always think first before agreeing to follow what someone tells me to do. And it really irks me when people just demand that I do something without explaining its necessity or benefits. Boy, will you get a snarky response from me if that's your leadership style!

• I'm a questioner—between a rule breaker and a rule follower lies the rule questioner who wants to know "why" the rule exists before deciding if she wants to follow it or break it. I always assumed all lawyers were questioners, but it might just be me.

• I get bored easily with redundant tasks. This one was a tough pill to swallow because I immediately labeled myself as flaky. Did I try to convince myself that I was a learner and naturally curious when instead I was always looking for the greener grass? Was I just noncommittal? Non-dependable? After I made the list, I would return to this dilemma many times, sometimes with compassion for myself, other times with a lot of judgment.

What this list gave me was a new vocabulary for expressing myself in the workplace. I began to lean into projects that energized me and fit my likes and at the same time, reduce the number of assignments I loathed. I did so by advocating for my own strengths and where I knew I would excel for the firm, and verbalizing the areas where I probably wouldn't do as good of a job as someone who loved that type of work. Admittedly, this type of career design holds a delicate balance. You can't just write a manifesto that says: "Here are my non-negotiables. This is the only work I will do. Everything else that doesn't fit squarely in the above will be rejected." That's just not how most jobs work. You have to approach it with a certain level of subtlety and diplomacy. But I promise it's possible to carve a day-to-day that you mostly enjoy if you are first willing to get introspective and list out your own likes, dislikes, and tolerates.

As I mentioned, after I returned to my firm, I essentially went back to working on the same cases I had before I left. Although it was exactly what I needed, it didn't take long for my brain to start getting antsy. Here is the truth about being an overachiever: monotony hits you hard. Just when you're getting in the groove and building back your confidence, bam! you start wondering if maybe you should try something new or do more with your life. It's important to pause and ask yourself what's the root of this feeling. If you are feeling pressured to measure up to someone's else idea for a career, or in a race with other lawyers to see who gets the biggest bonus, or spiraling because you believe you haven't achieved everything you thought you were supposed to achieve, then... breathe. Any action that stems from a panicked response to some outside factor will only lead to further dissatisfaction and feeling like you don't have agency over your decisions. Why? Because you're not choosing something out of genuine curiosity and self-initiated motivation; rather, you're relying on the outside world to tell you what to do. A learner trusts her unencumbered intuition to lead her to the next challenge, a challenge that she has voluntarily chosen for personal or professional growth, not exterior praise.

As I was asking myself what challenge I wanted to take on next, a new case came through our firm's doors. It was a mass litigation, spanning several states, that had been transferred to our firm after the initial firm that worked on this case had lost the first trial. The subject matter of this case was something that not many lawyers at our firm had experience in—I, for one, had never even heard of this topic. I was actually in the middle of a trial with the partner who "won" this bid for our firm. He was both nervous and excited and wouldn't stop talking about this work and what a tremendous opportunity it presented for our firm. He went around asking several senior associates if they wanted to work on the matter; all of them declined. Finally, he came to me and asked if I was interested. He told me that all the other associates explained their lack of experience in this area, their feelings of overwhelm with having to learn something new, and fear that they would disappoint the new client. I shared their concerns.

Yet something in me told me to accept the challenge. To learn something new. To see a different type of litigation. To expand my legal knowledge. To be a student again. To follow my curiosity. I didn't know a single thing about this practice area. But this eagerness to embrace my learner could only happen if I knew I worked at a company that supported me, with lawyers who would have my back. I would have never said yes if my former horrible boss had asked me. Now I felt professionally safe so to speak. More importantly, I was doing this because I *wanted* to, not because I felt pressured or guilted into agreeing. Although I respected the partner who asked me to join the team, I wasn't trying to get him to like me or give me a gold star. I was truly doing it for myself. My former perfectionist self had finally learned her lesson and chilled.

My story doesn't end here. If I had magically discovered myself all within a few short months of leaving my horrible in-house job, I wouldn't have enough material for a whole book! My chill lawyer experiment ebbed and flowed—some weeks I was really in the zone and feeling aligned; other times, I questioned everything and looked up jobs stocking shelves at Target (my idea of a totally chill job, which I am sure is actually not). I continued to experiment in my career for the next several years, including different practice areas and a very short stint at another law firm that ended up being the final nail in my legal career coffin. Although I ultimately realized that I was better suited in a career other than practicing law, I still work with lawyers daily and I know what it takes to create a sustainable, balanced, joyful, and uncomplicated career. Not only have I done it myself, but I have seen countless other lawyers create their own chill.

B. What Does Chill Look Like in a Lawyer?

When I was thinking about what inspired the chill lawyer theme of this book, I realized that it wasn't just me figuring out my own path in solitude without anyone to model what the law profession could look like. I actually had seen glimpses of happy, healthy, thriving lawyers who had discovered a way to make a stressful job work for them. In other words, they weren't passively bearing through legal practice, captive and without choice; they were active participants, molding their careers how it suited them. These lawyers (and by the way, there weren't many of them, but enough to give me hope!) had varying practice areas and spanned different age groups. Some were parents, some were second-career lawyers, and one had such a dedicated hobby that it was nearly a second job and yet he still had the ability to perform his high-visibility legal department leadership role. Yes, they were all different, but I noticed a common thread. That's not to say that every single individual possessed all of the qualities mentioned below, but these attributes showed up in sufficient quantities in each lawyer to lead me to this thesis.

I also want to disabuse you of the idea that in order to achieve this mindset, you must fully embody all of these qualities at all times. That's an impossible feat for us imperfect humans. However, the lesson here (as I hope is the lesson throughout the book) is that the goal is the activity itself, not the result. We can become so obsessed with the goal that we ignore the process which often gives us the biggest lesson. The point of this section isn't how to "achieve chill," since that is such a nebulous concept that your brain will immediately fight against it; rather, let's think about actions we can take today and tomorrow to garner feelings of chill. This activity-versus-result exercise can be spun into any aspect of your life. Instead of saying "I want to have a business," say "I am going to get 10 clients" as the latter statement indicates an action you can break down and do step by step today. Instead of saying "I want to be more productive," say "I am going to reduce my phone usage by an hour per day," which again signifies an action you can take now as opposed to a lofty goal of productivity. Learning to appreciate the process, the mundane day in and day out of progress, the minuscule gains—that's where the magic lies. If you focus on hitting a singular goal and you succeed, you win once. If you focus on doing the thing daily, even when it's hard or it doesn't feel like you're getting anywhere, then you achieve small wins every single day. In the long run, those add up to monumental wins.

So what does chill look like in a lawyer? In my experience, a chill lawyer first and foremost is confident in her abilities as not only a lawyer but as a human, a member of the local community, a friend, a partner, a creative, etc. That confidence is not expressed through cockiness or brashness, but rather through a self-assurance that she is deserving of a good life and a good career because she has worked hard and continues to hone her craft. She believes in herself, even when things get tough or don't work out the way she planned, because she knows that she is competent and able to do hard things.

How does an insecure overachiever gain this confidence? As the saying goes, "competence breeds confidence," so working backward, one should strive for skill and competence in whatever practice area he has chosen. The way he gets here is by repeatedly showing up for himself—in the good days, the bad days, the so-so days. Many lawyers have confidence issues because of long-standing perfectionism. If you've lived your entire life working toward perfect and beating yourself up every time you don't reach that impossible standard, then as you enter a profession that is so merciless about the smallest mistake, no wonder your confidence is constantly under attack. It's hard enough being a lawyer, but when you add in the performance pressure, the client pressure, the significant time invested daily into managing legal conflicts, it becomes a truly unhospitable work environment. I have met lawyers who were incredibly accomplished by any standard—former U.S. Supreme Court clerks, lawyers with nearly perfect trial records, and well-known legal luminaries—and every single one of these folks struggled with confidence.

Sergey's Story

Funny enough, one of the most confident lawyers I've ever met wasn't nearly as gifted as some of the others I mentioned. What he lacked in aptitude, he made up in his dedication to his practice as a personal injury attorney. Every day Sergey set aside an hour to deepen his legal expertise, calling it "Law School 2.0." Like many of us, Sergey didn't learn in law school the ins and outs of running a law firm, let alone working on contingency cases, getting clients, maintaining separate trust accounts, and all the intricacies associated with his job. But he felt a calling to serving injured people in his town, so he decided to teach himself. From the day he set up his firm until today—more than a decade later—Sergey religiously dedicates himself to learning a new topic.

He isn't a walking trivia winner or anything like that, but he has become one of the most knowledgeable personal injury attorneys you could ever find. He knows everything about the practice, and more importantly, he is so generous with the information he has gathered. I have heard of opposing counsel asking him for advice, as well as other personal injury attorneys who compete with him for clients. His confidence is completely self-developed. He felt that he was starting behind so many other accomplished lawyers and he knew the only way he could do his clients justice was by constantly and continually building up his competence as a lawyer.

I asked him if he'll ever do away with Law School 2.0 and he immediately waved me off, rattling all the new things he looks forward to learning, like using artificial intelligence to support his practice and the ways in which non-lawyers could assist on cases in order to decrease his clients' fees. His thirst for information has made him such an invaluable resource and an all-around great person. He's not only the lawyer you'd want in your corner, but also the one you'd hope for across the table.

A chill lawyer is also healthy, and by healthy, I don't mean able-bodied or without any illness. I am referring to a person who is striving for a healthy and balanced life, understanding that we all go through seasons in life and sometimes we are less healthy and less balanced than we'd like to be. A healthy lawyer prizes his sleep, rest, and time away from work. He knows that those aren't weaknesses or an inability to cope; rather, they are the very fuel necessary for a long and productive career. A healthy lawyer nourishes his body because he knows that it is the vehicle he will be in for life. He protects his time spent on movement, stretching, or engaging in an active hobby.

Len's Story

I used to work with a lawyer who was well into his 60s and worked out every single day, including during months-long trials. I asked him if he had always exercised and he told me that he didn't start until he was 50 because his doctor told him that he wouldn't make it to his 90s (like his father, who is now a centenarian) if he kept up his lifestyle. My face dropped as I naively asked if it was hard beginning an exercise routine at such an old age,[12] and he responded without missing a beat: "Not as hard as it would've been if I died before my dad." This man was a partner at a large law firm, a trial lawyer, a huge business developer, a husband, a dad, a grandpa, proud owner of two beautiful purebred dogs, etc. He had an incredibly full life and given his rather advanced age, he could've just said enough is enough. But he realized that good health wasn't just going to happen to him; he had to make it a priority.

The bottom line is that it's never too late to start moving your body and, as you will see in the next chapter, I don't even mean hitting the gym and lifting weights like this lawyer in his 60s. It's actually much simpler, but we often stop ourselves from doing the simple because we make it out to be hard in our minds.

Earlier in the book I talked about Tara Mohr's reference to the inner mentor that lives inside all of us. As lawyers, we're often advised to find mentors who will guide us along the way and support us in learning about the legal profession. While they are valuable resources, you shouldn't rely on another person to influence your career decisions. What works for another lawyer in her professional life may not work for you and even if that person has your best interests, she doesn't have to live your life—only you do.

Your intuition is the only voice that's truly yours. Sometimes that voice doesn't tell us exactly what we want to hear, sometimes it's the only thing that makes sense. The point isn't to question it or to try to find an alternative answer (which is a big ask for lawyers, I know). You just have to let it say what it says, then allow it to unfold in your life. Following your intuition doesn't require that you stop heeding all advice and throw caution to the wind; rather, it nudges you to question what others tell you, what's expected of you, and how things have always been done.

Another bonus of learning to listen to your inner mentor is the realization that both praise *and* reproach are woefully unhelpful external factors that we have learned to internalize over a lifetime. What do I mean by that? Remember when you were a kid and you had a particular hobby that you loved doing above all else? Whether it was drawing or kicking a ball around or pretending you were a samurai with a toy sword, you didn't care whether you were any good or whether your parents commended you for your excellent passion. You just did it because you loved it. As you grew older, the pressure started building up: is this an activity you will excel in? Will this become the sport you play? Will it get you a scholarship? Are you a child prodigy? If the answer was no, then you were kindly encouraged to stop wasting time and instead focus on schoolwork or some other hobby that was deemed acceptable by your parents (and society).

These early experiences that we all share impress upon us the notion that activities are only good if we excel in them, and by extension, *we* as humans are only worthy if we receive praise. Thus begins the never-ending quest into adulthood to seek approval and avoid criticism. We all do it. We do it as young adults chasing good grades and friends who like us, we do it as working adults constantly trying to impress our bosses and co-workers, and it really never ends. It's human. It's not something we can altogether banish.

But think about something you really love, whether it's an activity, a hobby, a movie genre, or anything that brings you pure joy. Something that you keep to yourself or you don't engage in frequently because you're afraid of how you might be judged. Something that, if you could transport back to those unbridled kid days, you would do and enjoy tremendously. Now think of all the 1.3 million lawyers out there who also have a hidden love that they too had to abandon in favor of approval from you and other lawyers. This is one of the few aspects of life that connects all of us. And think about how much richer all our lives would be if we allowed our inner wisdom to guide us back to those joyful activities.

One mental shift that has helped me reduce (albeit not completely remove) my fixation with praise and criticism is understanding that, at its core, everything is just feedback. People around us give feedback all day long, whether it is praise, criticism, anger, agreement, indifference, support, silence, obsession, understanding, etc. This feedback is based on numerous factors like how the person is feeling in that moment, what other thoughts and emotions this person is going through that day, what lens this person is seeing your action through, and so many more. Most of the time the feedback we receive is less about us and more about the person giving it. So instead of taking every piece of feedback as the gospel or the absolute truth, I started viewing it as just information. My thought process goes something like this:

I say or do something → Jamie hears or sees my act →

Jamie processes this information through his
own life experiences, biases, etc. →

Jamie then gives me feedback → I take his
feedback as information, without the need to
approve it, reject it, or act on it in any way

The end.

I know this seems easier said than done, but I encourage you
to try it with just a small act first. Allow someone to give you
information on something that isn't integral to your life (avoid big
questions like "Am I a good wife?") and try to see the perspective
of the person giving you the feedback without putting value on the
comment itself. This is where your intuition will come in: if you
know deep down that you speak and act from a good place, no
amount of praise *or* criticism can affect that inner feeling. If you are
living your truth, no one can enhance or diminish it.

Mariah's Story

I knew a lawyer who started out her legal career like a rocket,
quickly mastering her practice area and making a name for herself
as a go-to litigator shortly after passing the bar exam. Five years
in, she crashed and burned. No, I'm not being mean-spirited in
my description. She literally began to drop the ball on her cases
and practicing so sloppily that those around her were befuddled.
When she left the practice of law to get her real estate license,
other lawyers naturally assumed that she couldn't hack it and
that the jig was finally up. I caught up with her about a year into
her real estate job and she was beaming. She had such poise and
confidence, but most importantly, her new career came so natural
to her. She told me that she felt like a complete misfit as a lawyer,

so she tried the old "fake it 'til you make it" approach, which seemed to work until it didn't. The more she tried to force herself into her legal job, the harder it became, and she started to miss deadlines, make huge blunders in her motions, and generally disserve her clients.

I asked her what made her decide to leave and go into real estate. Her answer was so simple that I nearly didn't believe her: she looked inward and asked herself what would little Mariah have wanted older Mariah to do with her life? That's it, that was the question. She then remembered how much she loved helping her mom in her home decorating business when she was a kid, always following her around as she staged homes before they would go on the market. She would always ask her mom if the home she had staged sold, and her mom would indulge her and give her details about the listing price, the negotiations, etc. This is what lit Mariah up as a kid and, it turns out, this is what she felt she was meant to do with her career.

It has now been several years since Mariah got into real estate and she is still as passionate and driven as she was when she first made the switch. She didn't launch into space only to crash and burn like she did as a lawyer. Because she doesn't have to fake enjoying real estate; she truly does.

I am sure you know lawyers like Mariah who seem to have it all from the outside only to one day abandon it for some other occupation that to you, might not make sense. Maybe these lawyers haven't had to suffer the public humiliation that Mariah did, maybe they were able to get ahead of it by listening to their intuition and changing course before the deception caught up. If you know a lawyer with this story, do yourself a solid and have a conversation with him or her. You will learn more than you can imagine.

Another aspect of a chill lawyer is being a lifelong learner and with that comes the acceptance that we never truly master anything. We are constantly evolving, learning from our successes as well as our mistakes. We seemingly put a lot of emphasis on learning as lawyers, but in reality, what we teach lawyers is that they should aspire for excellence. Excellence by its very definition signals an end of the learning process and the achievement of the very best. I always like to remind lawyers that we practice law, we don't perfect it. It's a practice, a constant education, an acknowledgment that we will never know it all, but we should continue to learn as much as we can. A chill lawyer sees the beauty—not the despair—in these statements.

There is a saying about the legal profession that is so accurate, I can't even think of anything else to add to it: Being a lawyer is like a cake-eating contest where the prize is more cake. Some of you may have experienced the paradox of becoming the go-to lawyer for a partner or a client or an entire practice group (bless you!) and finding yourself unable to turn off the faucet of work that keeps streaming in. Some lawyers regale in this feeling of mastery and accomplishment and want to ride it all the way to retirement. If you have chosen this particular expertise, it can be incredibly rewarding. I would argue that even if you completely adore the proficiency you've acquired, you will still need to learn to say no and become choosier; otherwise, you will eventually drown. Here's the larger point:

Developing an expertise leads to . . .

↑ Increased demands on your time for said expertise

↓ Lessened ability to turn down opportunities

↓ Less time to learn anything else

While you might become the foremost expert of cyber attacks or farming law, you do so at the cost of hours that you could dedicate to learning and growing as a person. Don't get me wrong: I am a huge fan of finding your career spark and going after it at the detriment of all other career options, as you will see later in this book. However, I don't believe that we truly ever master anything, and as such, we should continue learning. The choice here isn't between becoming an expert or forever dooming yourself to a jack-of-all-trades career; rather, the vulnerability in this position lies in the loss of capacity to decline any opportunity presented to you that appears to be related to your expertise (which then leads to saying yes to too many things) *and* the consequential inability to dedicate time to upskilling in other ways.

Former lawyer turned host of the ubiquitous podcast "The Good Life Project," Jonathan Fields, frequently talks about his scientist persona. He's endlessly curious and loves tinkering with new ideas and projects. In fact, the reason he created his podcast over a decade ago was partly due to his obsession with understanding what makes people tick and how they're able to build lives and careers they love.[13] He was asked in a recent interview why he keeps going after making nearly 1,000 episodes and he responded with: "The quest is kind of consistently who do I want to keep learning from?"[14] For Fields, it's not just about mastering his craft or continuing to expand beyond his millions of listeners, it's about discovering new ways of thinking.

The final piece of my chill lawyer maxim is living light or, better put, keeping a lightness in your daily life. You know those cheesy throw pillows and wall décor that appeared in every millennial woman's house circa 2007: Live, laugh, love? That's basically the inspiration behind this pillar. Look, life can be hard. We're surrounded by horrible events that seemingly occur with increased frequency and with larger death tolls than ever. We experienced a global pandemic, which seemed unthinkable several years ago. There are so many wrongs we live with as a society, so much pain, so much unfairness, so much out of our control. How do we keep a lightness in our hearts in the face of darkness?

During a particularly trying time in my life, I tried to get myself to meditate. So I installed an app on my phone that guided me through short meditations each morning and every day it started with a mantra. On the morning of January 1 at the start of a new year, my phone pinged and said: "Always believe that something wonderful is about to happen." What an excellent little thought! This is what distinguishes humans from most animals: our ability to think about the future and dream. As a species, we have a marvelous inclination toward optimism. Even when we experience horrible setbacks, our ability to look to the future with hope and create a new life for ourselves and those around us is nothing short of remarkable. Not everyone is born an optimist, but we can all find evidence of things working in our favor. Sometimes I believe that optimism is simply recalling a lucky situation and convincing yourself it can happen again. There's no magic or mysticism to it; just a simple belief that good things will come your way.

Javaris's Story

A friend of mine from law school was an avid guitar player and part of a small band. Just from watching him on stage, you could tell that he was having a blast. He played all throughout law school and continued on with the same band as a practicing lawyer. Javaris told me that, as a lawyer he often felt like he had to be someone else—someone professional, knowledgeable, zealous—but as a guitar player, he only had to be himself. Despite not feeling like himself, Javaris became a wonderful criminal defense attorney.

A few years into his practice, he learned that his mom had cancer. As she lived in Jamaica, Javaris made the difficult decision to cut back his practice to part-time and travel back and forth to help his mom with her cancer treatment. He told me that he didn't think twice about this decision, as he knew it was what he had to do. He continued representing clients between his trips to Jamaica while acting as his mom's full-time caregiver. The most striking part to me, however, was that Javaris never stopped playing his guitar, lugging it through the airports on all of his trips. So in addition to his law practice and being with his mom through her yearlong cancer treatment, Javaris played with his band when he was home and solo in small venues when he was in Jamaica.

Playing guitar is what brought him lightness during this dark period of his life. It's what kept him going when his mom's side effects were so bad that she couldn't go to the bathroom by herself or when his opposing counsel pulled jerk moves like unilaterally setting hearings and ignoring his out of office message. Again, he repeated to me that he felt most like himself when playing the guitar. Of course, his mom loved him playing too. More than that though, every time he strapped on his guitar, an automatic smile blasted across his face. Even when he was tired and sad and desperate over his mom's lack of progress, he never faked a smile with that guitar on.

Javaris's mom unfortunately succumbed to her cancer. He played her favorite song on his guitar at her funeral. When he returned to his full-time practice, he reflected on this trying experience: no, he didn't regret his decisions and while he wished he had more time with his mom, he was forever grateful that he never stopped playing guitar. It was and is more than a hobby; rather, his guitar represents an extension of his soul, a third limb, a figurative trekking pole to guide him in life.

Thinking back on Javaris's story, I realize that I too always keep a lightness in my heart. Sometimes it's a very quiet voice in the midst of chaos, other times, it's loud and boisterous and likes to make friends. It's not easy to be light, but like a muscle, the lightness gets stronger every time you acknowledge it. I would be an asshole if I didn't acknowledge that mental illness can render some incapable of simply finding their lightness and that, despite valiant efforts, they can't just will themselves to feel light. While I wish for nothing more than for everyone to be able to experience what Javaris and I feel, I realize the impossibility of that feat. I do want to urge all lawyers to find small joys in their daily lives.

And with that, we have to start small. Notice the sun coming into your bedroom in the morning. Feel your chest expand and contract as you breathe in fresh oxygen to nourish your organs. Savor that first sip of coffee or tea. Marvel at the squirrels or birds outside of your window, those energetic little acrobats. Look at the clouds: are they fluffy and slow-moving, shallow and rapidly changing shapes and direction, white or gray? Do the trees around your home and office look the same today as they did yesterday? There is so much going on around us that we simply fail to notice. Worse, we don't see it change and evolve. Observing the impermanence around us can make us happier by reminding us that nothing lasts forever and life is always shifting. Today's bad mood might go away tomorrow. The crappy job won't last forever. The unhealthy relationship will meet its demise. This concept is more digestible if you start paying attention to how nature transforms all around you. It's a small habit, free and not very time consuming.

II

Choosing the Chill Path

Dr. Andrew Huberman, host of the popular podcast "Huberman Lab" and professor at the Stanford School of Medicine, lists the following six crucial components for self-care and health: sleep and sleep routine, sunlight, movement, nutrition, social connection, and stress control.[15] Although these seem self-evident, Dr. Huberman suggests that we must achieve each one within a 24-hour period for optimal health. In other words, if you get great sleep on Monday through Friday, but you don't move or feed your body with proper nutrition daily, you're still operating at a deficiency. You can't overcompensate in one area and neglect other aspects in hopes that they will balance out. Each component is integral and independent of the others. While it may seem daunting to even try, the research is clear that lawyers absolutely need it. We are living in a crisis of poor habits for lawyers.

Dr. Huberman's research isn't meant to be discouraging but I can appreciate that it seems like a lot to do, so I have broken it down into three broader parts: body, mind, and spirit. I am not perfect at attending to these three aspects on a daily basis, but the goal for me—as it should be for all of us—is to try each day to give ourselves a small win for our bodies, minds, and spirit. That's it. Study after study shows that we create sustainable habits by taking one small step at a time versus promising ourselves a hugely monumental goal, then disappointing ourselves when we fail to go from 0 to 100. As former lawyer and incredible writer/happiness guru Gretchen Rubin says, "What you do every day matters more than what you do once in a while."[16] So running a triathlon once a year is less important for your health than walking daily. The inverse is also true: overeating one time will not suddenly reverse all the progress you've made toward eating healthy on a daily basis.

So let's take it a step at a time and focus on each activity versus setting ourselves up for failure by choosing unsurmountable goals.

A. Chill Body

I start off our journey together toward chill with the body because study after study shows that our bodies store every trauma, every stressor, and every difficult moment. And frankly, it's much easier to master your body than to master your brain. If you are in a place where you want to take charge of your career and free up your mental resources so that you can be more intentional about your next steps, I promise you that the easiest place to begin and where you will see the most progress is through moving your body. Rather than diving in headfirst into a job search or a frantic internet search about alternative careers for lawyers, you first must allow your body to release the tension and stress you've been carrying around this whole time. For many busy lawyers, movement and proper nutrition seem like a hard hill to climb, so we will do it step by step, adding one component every week for six weeks.

Positive body movement also impacts the brain in a positive way. Research shows that there are so many brain-based benefits to exercise, including:

- Release of dopamine: the neurotransmitter associated with focus, motivation, and pleasure;

- Increase of norepinephrine: a chemical that supports stress response;

- Additional blood supply to the brain: promotes the growth of new neurons that can improve cognition and memory;

- Surge of serotonin: it stabilizes mood, regulates anxiety, and helps cognitive functions.[17]

In his groundbreaking book *Atomic Habits,* James Clear writes about what it takes to create and sustain new habits. According to Clear, the easiest way to begin a new habit is by allowing yourself two minutes to work on it daily.[18] Every big goal can be broken down in small parts. Clear offers the example of writing a book as a very difficult goal for most people because it requires a tremendous amount of effort and dedication. So he proposes a breakdown: first you write one sentence, then one paragraph, then one page, and so on. Building this new habit takes only two minutes a day.[19] What eventually happens is that your brain is on autopilot: every day it knows that it will write for two minutes and eventually, it wants to write for longer. The same example can be used for working out, walking, running, meditating, or starting a yoga practice.

Below I have set out some examples of beginning a new workout routine with simple and easily achievable steps:

Week 1: Begin gentle morning stretches. If you need some inspiration, check out Yoga with Adrienne on YouTube for her beginner-friendly yoga series.

Week 2: Add in a long walk once a week and 10-minute walks daily. The best time to walk is as soon as you wake up because it boosts energy and slowly eases your brain into the day.

Week 3: Add one vegetable to each lunch and each dinner. Just one! I told you we would start easy.

Week 4: Try one new exercise program that you've always been curious about, but never really did before. If you live in a bigger metropolitan area, you probably can't throw a quarter without hitting a fitness studio, so start there. Most studios offer a free or deeply discounted first class.

Week 5: Go to sleep 30 minutes to one hour earlier than usual *and* wake up 30 minutes to one hour earlier. This is a tough one because most of us feel shackled to our current sleep schedules (no matter how vicious they actually are), but truly, anyone can try going to bed 30 minutes earlier and setting the alarm for 30 minutes before the usual wake-up time. You can slowly keep pushing these times back by 30 minutes until your body gets accustomed to the new sleep routine.

Week 6: Pick two days during the week where you either commit to doing the new exercise program you tried in week 4 *or* choose a different exercise program you like. Try to spend at least 30 minutes on each of the two days with this exercise.

At this point in your health journey, all these new habits might start adding up and it might feel difficult. We often begin new endeavors with excitement and curiosity, but we eventually forget those emotions as things become harder. My high school volleyball coach was tough—not in a mean way, but in a "I won't let you give up way." Before difficult drills or back-to-back practices, she would say "I know this is hard, but we're going to do it anyway." Sometimes that's exactly what we need to say to ourselves: it's hard, but do it anyway. We are so much stronger than we allow our brains to realize. It's almost like a hidden secret we keep until we need it.

Out of all these exercises (and they are all beneficial in their own ways), nothing comes more naturally to us humans than walking. After all, we developed as a species by going from four legs to two and we continue to develop from crawling babies to walking adults. But we take walking for granted—we literally see it as a way to get from one place to another, like from our bed to our car to our couch. Walking just for the sake of walking, however, is a sacred practice. Writer Sarah Wilson talks about the French concept of a flaneur in her book *This One Wild and Precious Life*, which roughly translates to someone who strolls about or saunters.[20] Another term for it is a boulevardier, literally someone who walks around boulevards. The concept was made famous by the Parisian intellectual elite who realized that ambling about the city offered not only exercise but a time to observe the world around them and ponder life's questions. The whole purpose of these walks then became a way to explore parts of the city that one is familiar with, but not too familiar, and to walk with the sole purpose of thinking and observing rather than arriving at a destination. In Wilson's words "When we walk, we have the emotional space to discern where the hell right and wrong land for us. . . Walking is a forward motion. Love, yearning, and all the optimistic endeavors of the human experience are also forward motions. When we walk we attune to these positive forces."[21]

I live near the beautiful Tampa Bay, which boasts one of the longest continuously running sidewalks in the country that curves around the bay, allowing breathtaking water views and frequent encounters with the resident dolphins, manatees, turtles, and sometimes even a wandering gator. I am ashamed to admit that I didn't seriously start walking on this trail until the pandemic when I felt suffocated by all the virus talk, depressing news, and Zoom meetings. But I just started one morning, with no expectation that this would become a *thing* and without tracking how far I was going. The walk itself was so peaceful. I can hardly put into words how both calming and energizing it felt. I went again the next day, then the next day, and four years later, I walk nearly every morning. At this point, I would rather skip a workout than my walk. It has become so ingrained in my daily routine, in who I am as a person (I actually identify as someone who walks every morning), and in my mental well-being that I can't conceive dropping it.

In addition to the obvious perks of a daily walk, I also encountered what Wilson refers to as the "morality of walking."[22] The number of dilemmas and sticky questions I've resolved during my walks is astounding. It's as if my brain unravels all the tied-up thoughts as I tack on miles and sorts them out without much effort on my part. Nowadays I often feel like I can't think clearly unless I am walking. It has been a practice that has spurred creativity, problem-solving, compassion, understanding, learning, and even some good old-fashioned raging at what is going on in the world. Sometimes you need a little rage, especially when you find yourself in a very calming environment. I've written two books during my walks, I designed my business during my walks, I learned how to be a better friend and mentor, and I decided what matters to me in life *and* how to pursue it. I have benefited from walking so much that I hope my headstone will say something like "She walked through life and now she will walk through death" or something a bit more joyful.

Why am I rambling so much about walking? Because, like many other forms of movement, it offers more than just a physical activity. People boast about the trance-like feel of a yoga class, the deep focus during a CrossFit® workout, and the single-minded pursuit of a basket during a pickup game. Movement forces our brains to focus on the task at hand while simultaneously offering space for us to think and create. It's almost as if the physical movement forces our brain to deviate from usual thought patterns and think differently.

B. Chill Mind

Arthur Brooks, Harvard University professor on happiness and author of "Build the Life You Want," has a simple recipe for happiness: enjoyment + satisfaction + purpose.[23] The first ingredient, enjoyment, is best shared with others in order to create memorable experiences as opposed to dangerous vices. The second ingredient, satisfaction, lies in the strive from struggle to achievement. Humans, Brooks points out, "need to struggle, we need to strive, we need to sacrifice, we even need pain in our lives, because that's actually how we earn something."[24] Purpose is the trickiest component to happiness because it is inherently subjective. What drives me and gives my life meaning may not be the same for you. But in order to find your own compass, you must learn to consistently check in with yourself and evaluate if the compass is pointing you in the direction you want to go.

For many of us, no conversation about happiness can take place without involving the thing that so often makes us unhappy: our jobs. How can one facet of our lives derive so much stress and discontent, while also generating feelings of accomplishment, fulfillment, and pride? As much as we may want to cast aside our jobs as "not who we really are," let's face it, as lawyers our identities are very much intertwined with what we do. Part of it is the snobby profession we've chosen, but I believe that a big piece of that is deeply entrenched in who we are as people and why we were drawn to become lawyers in the first place. Setting aside the philosophical debate, many lawyers find themselves at some point in their careers dissatisfied and disheartened, wondering what their next step should be. I myself have been there several times over my decade-long legal journey, so I want to offer some advice and support.

When thinking about a career pivot or going for another job, most lawyers I have spoken to generally take one of two approaches: they either just take the next job hoping that this would be "it" or they obsessively research alternatives praying for one to jump out as the next obvious thing for them to do. I've been in both situations and perhaps you have too. When I had enough of my very comfortable firm job—the one that I had started out in as a first-year lawyer and eventually returned to after my in-house stint—I began to casually look for other jobs, not really knowing what exactly I wanted to do next. I came upon another firm position that sounded vaguely interesting, applied, had the interviews, got the job, and accepted it without truly giving it a thought as to what exactly I was hoping to gain in this new position. I distinctly remember the managing partner asking during my interview why I wanted to work there, while I struggled not to answer, "I don't know, but I'm hoping to find out." It was essentially a lateral move to another firm in a practice area I thought I liked. Well, as it turned out, I didn't love it. Not only did I not love it, I actually loved it *way less* than my prior firm job. Stupid move, right? In hindsight though, we make the best decisions we can with the information and the thoughts we have at the time. Like everything else, it was a good lesson and an experience that led me to the next phase in my career search and the second option I mentioned above: research.

After what became my third different job as a lawyer, I started to think that perhaps practicing law wasn't in the cards for me. Honestly, that idea wasn't scary to me. I had practiced law for over seven years at that point, so I didn't believe I was throwing in the towel. Instead, I felt like I had given it a fair shot—both in a law firm setting and in-house—and ultimately it was time for me to try something else. I thought I could figure out the next thing in a few months simply by immersing myself in researching alternative law careers. I read all the books, listened to all the podcasts, took all the personality quizzes, read all the blogs and whatever else I could my hands on. And nothing. Actually, not nothing: there was seemingly an infinite number of jobs I could pursue, which left me completely overwhelmed and unable to make a decision.

Neither option works in the long run because both are premised on the idea that the dream job or the right career will magically appear out of the blue. And you will know it's the right thing to do and all the stars will align, and you will sail into the sunset never again to think about this stuff again. Both options trick you into believing that there is *one* right job for you, when in reality, there are likely several different professions you could take on, each with its own pluses and minuses. The truth is that even the most perfect match will present some downsides that you have to put up with, or job BS as I like to call it. All jobs have a level of BS that is entrenched in their daily schedule. You get to decide what type of BS you can tolerate.

I want to highlight something that I believe isn't discussed often: tradeoffs. Every career decision (really, every significant decision) you make will have tradeoffs. It is quite simply hopeless to try to avoid any downsides whatsoever in favor of pure gains. In our current world—full of endless options, too many options one might argue—I find that many lawyers spin their wheels to avoid making decisions because they can't suffer to accept any tradeoffs. They're so mesmerized by all the possibilities that it becomes impossible to make a choice, accept the drawbacks, and charge on. This is where lawyers get stuck in indecision. It becomes more comfortable, seemingly less costly and certainly less scary to stay in current misery as opposed to take a risk. But by default, staying in your current situation means that you *are* accepting certain tradeoffs. It might not feel like you're choosing these tradeoffs, but any inaction is simply choosing the current status quo.

Which brings me back to my "Likes/dislikes/tolerates" list I mentioned earlier. All career coaches worth their salt will tell you that the only way to figure out your next career move is to know thyself. No one can make that decision for you, even if you give them all your requirements in advance and the results of every personality or aptitude test you've ever taken. No one can tell you: "Here, this is exactly what you should be doing for the rest of your life." Only you can solve this dilemma. You have to engage in the introspective and yes, sometimes lengthy and frustrating process of listing out every task you like to do, every task you absolutely dislike (which actually becomes the job BS you can't take), and everything you might be able to tolerate (or the trade-offs you're willing to accept). Before you can figure out a job or new profession that suits you, you have to know yourself.

So many lawyers bring up finances as a reason not to pursue their true career dreams. The legal profession has done an excellent job marketing the salaries of lawyers as a crutch. Yes, we use it as a crutch not just to stay in jobs we hate, but to continue practicing law. This book isn't about leaving the law because many of you are meant to be lawyers and you love the profession, yet you still tolerate work environments that you don't need to tolerate and people you don't need to tolerate. Lawyers catastrophize when it comes to financial decisions as either continuing in their current, miserable yet high-paying jobs or ending up homeless, living under a bridge. There is no in-between.

Bill Perkins (not a lawyer, in case you're sensing a theme in this book) writes in his mind-blowing book *Die with Zero* about the mindset he developed around money and life energy. He explains that most high-achieving professionals hoard money at the cost of life experiences in fear that they will run out, despite the research showing that the vast majority of wealth in this country is in the hands of people aged 75 and older.[25] In other words, unless you are living in poverty, the chances of outliving your money are incredibly slim. In fact, most professionals see a compound increase in their wealth as they get older. And it mostly goes by unnoticed. Think about it: when is the last time you celebrated a paycheck or a bonus? When is the last time you looked at your savings or investments with joy—not because of the amounts, but because of the life experiences it affords you? Perkins asks the question: "How do you maximize the value of your experiences in order to make the most out of your one life?" Although posited as a financial book, *Die with Zero* is really masterclass in how to live a good life.

If you need more convincing in the form of actual numbers, Perkins offers the example of a fictional 45-year-old single person earning $60,000 per year. This amount is vastly below what most lawyers earn, but let's just stick with his example. This person hopes to retire at age 65, so she puts away $16,000 per year in savings and investments. For the sake of simplicity, assume that her house is paid off and valued at $450,000. With these numbers in mind, she will retire with a total net worth of $770,000. If she continues her general spending habits upon retirement—which is unlikely for most folks as living expenses go down in retirement—and lives to age 85, she will have left behind $130,000.[26] Think about what she could have done with that money had she known it would outlive her.

Again, this is an overly simplified financial example that is not even adjusted for inflation, but the point remains true in more complex situations: most of us live in financial scarcity, constantly afraid that we will run out of money and thus delaying our enjoyment of life for the sake of saving for retirement or saving for a rainy day. Neither Perkins nor I suggest that you should spend every dime or empty out your 401(k) to travel around the world, but you should take an honest look at your finances and figure out what is the best use of not just your money, but how you want to spend your life. Is it a new job? A business venture? A sabbatical? Investing in your kids' education? Whatever your goal is, it is far more likely that you have enough to start working toward it now as opposed to waiting for that someday to come.

Back to the variety of career paths you could embark on, there is a universal truth among all: deciding what you want to spend your working hours on and pursuing that will necessarily require that you say "no" to other alluring options. There is a story in coaching circles that is often attributed to Warren Buffet, although his involvement is unclear, but it goes like this:

> A very successful person is working on long-term goal planning and cannot figure out which priorities to focus his attention on first, and which to follow second and third, and so on. A close friend of his suggests that he list the 25 most important items that he wants to accomplish in his life by order of significance. This person takes a long time to create his list, carefully ordering and reordering each item. Finally, he has the full list and he shows it to his friend, hoping for some advice. His friend says: "Good. Now remove the last 20 items in your list and only focus on the first five because those are the only

goals you will truly be able to devote yourself to and therefore accomplish. The rest are just distractions."

There are two lessons here. First, much as we'd like to try, we really can only masterfully achieve a few things in life. Sure, we can get pretty close to completing other goals or we can dabble in a bunch of different hobbies and work assignments, but dedicating ourselves to a select number of priorities will always win out. The second lesson is that the difficulty in navigating life is learning to say no to things that we actually really want and might enjoy. That number six or number seven item on your list is *really* close to number five or number four and those aspirations will *really* tempt you throughout life. When given the option between focusing on something you've decided is a top-five priority versus trying something that is pretty close to that top five, you have to learn to say no to that other cool, but ultimately not-top-five item.

The overlap between things you must do and things you'd like to do is where Greg McKeown's concept of essentialism lies. McKeown, who (wisely) dropped out of law school to focus on writing about productivity, calls it "the disciplined pursuit of less" and he teaches that in order to live the life that we want to live, we must say no to everything that we have decided is not essential to us.[27] As you might imagine, this is a highly personal decision that involves introspection, thoughtfulness, and removing all of society's noise about what we should do or should want. If you struggle with prioritizing and managing the allotted hours you have each day, remember that:

Time management is really attention management.

Start paying close attention to how you spend your time and most importantly, who decides how you spend your time. When we don't consciously choose what we do daily, someone else makes that choice for us. Most of us like to believe that we're in charge of our schedule when in reality, we're frequently shackled by other people's priorities. And we allow it. Instead of trying to manipulate your calendar or become more productive (i.e., cram more shit in an already overflowing pot), think about where you want your attention to go. Do you want your attention on that recurring 30-minute staff meeting where everyone just goes around and complains about how busy they are *or* do you want 30 minutes to yourself to just plan out your upcoming week? Do you want your attention on that lunch meeting with so-and-so's business contact who might one day give your firm work *or* would you rather take a walking lunch outside in the sunshine? Would you rather proofread this agreement for the umpteenth time to ease your anxiety over a potential misplaced comma *or* should you use this time to write out an actually doable personal marketing plan for next year that will take your career where you want it?

It's not simply about getting rid of things on your to-do list just for the sake of clearing your calendar—it's about deciding where you want to focus your attention and going after it at the cost of all other insignificant tasks. The best way I've found to do this is to track hour by hour an entire week. Start with the moment you wake up and finish with the time you close your eyes. Be as honest and detailed as possible in this exercise. Along with identifying each task, you should also note who is deciding that you are doing it. The results will be clarifying and utterly humbling as you will realize that (1) you spend a whole lot of time doing things you don't really want to do for reasons that aren't exactly apparent, and (2) you've relinquished your decision-making to other people and are now bound by their schedules. If this revelation upsets you, that's a great start!

In their enlightening book *Make Time: How to Focus on What Matters Every Day*, former Google product designers Jake Knapp and John Zeratsky write about the default state: a preselected option that you have no say in but that you automatically get enrolled into every time you engage in a certain activity, like buying a new phone that has default notifications programmed to alert you of new emails, new text messages, etc. or starting a new job where the default culture is the more meetings, the better.[28] Changing these default settings takes intention and effort, so most people just give in and allow the default to dictate their lives. Do you think that the scrolling feature on most social media apps or the automatic start of the next episode after you finish an episode on streaming platforms are accidental? These features literally bet on your acquiescence to the default settings—they know you won't take the time to change anything.

Like McKeown, Knapp and Zeratsky propose that willpower and productivity aren't the solutions; rather, we must choose a few things that matter to us individually, focus our attention and energy on *just* those things until we accomplish them, then rinse and repeat.[29] For instance, if your goal is to write a book (like it was for me), then you have to choose this activity with regular occurrence—at the price of not completing other items—until you've reached your goal. Or if you want to get a new job, you must devote certain time on a regular basis to this endeavor until you get a new job. It's quite simple in theory, but it's certainly not easy. Why? Because it's easier to go along with all the meetings already set on your calendar and with your routine of staying up until midnight binging whatever show is supposedly a must-watch and with your default food consumption and your default lack of regular exercise and so on. But are any of these choices ones that, given the chance *right now*, you would actually willingly pick? If your answer is no, then you know what to do. It won't be easy, but it is simple.

Returning to the point of careers, I've coached quite a few lawyers at this point and the biggest complaint about their careers is that they feel a major disconnect between who they are (or were before becoming lawyers) and what they are expected to do in their jobs. And I don't mean a huge moral quandary about whether they can ethically represent a certain client; I am talking about something more personal, something deeper, something that is hard to put into words. It's the feeling of leaving part of who you really are at the door before walking into work. It's the habit of thinking with your lawyer brain before your human brain when making both personal and career choices. It's almost like a lack of trust in your own instincts because the rational part of your brain has taken over the decision-making process and she is bossy as hell.

> We have trained so hard to think like lawyers that
> we've forgotten how to think like ourselves.

Our brains like patterns. They've evolved over thousands of years to try to predict what will happen next based on prior experiences. That's usually a good thing—that's how we know not to eat that poisonous berry or try to pet a wild lion. But this pattern thinking also creates limitations and fears. If left to its own devices, the brain's gonna brain and it'll keep you safe (and bored and unfulfilled and stagnant) forever. We all think unhelpful thoughts, we all feel shame, we all suffer from indecision and regret and wanting what other people have. There is nothing inherently wrong with any of these thoughts, except when they act to prevent you from living a full life. Learn how to watch your thoughts. What do I mean by that? There is power in understanding that not every thought that buzzes around our head is a fact. Actually, most aren't. Thoughts are filtered through our past experiences, our biases, our current mood, the way we've been socialized since the time we were children, etc. Thoughts pick up these little tidbits of information that we store in our subconscious before surfacing to our conscious minds. They are not raw facts; they are loaded with all kinds of data, some of it true, some not so true. The lesson is to observe your thoughts without attaching truth or weight to any particular one, no matter how factual it seems.

C. Chill Spirit

Most lawyers don't think of themselves as being creative. In fact, most of us were drawn to law school in part due to its penchant for reason, rationality, truth-seeking, and factuality. We are desperately searching for *the* case, *the* answer, *the* precedent, when in practice, we know that "it all depends." This binary school of thought may be what we learn in law school, but it's not how law practice really works. Think about what clients are asking of you as a lawyer: they want to know how to best navigate super complex legal issues. They want you to offer them legally defensible ideas and paths to getting to an optimal result. Very often, that requires a lawyer to think through several different options and come up with at least one or, more likely, a few ways to accomplish the client's goal. Now, the lawyer may benefit from a roadmap from a previous case with similar facts, but even then, every client has different needs, risk appetites, objectives, budgets, etc. The lawyer still has to use judgment and problem-solving skills on every single matter. That, my friends, is creativity.

Like perseverance and emotional intelligence, creativity is a muscle that needs to be developed and strengthened. We are all innately creative beings. Every single one of us craves to make something new, to think through cool ideas, to appreciate art in all of its forms. But life makes us stagnant, practical, and jaded, so we forget how to behave creatively. In her inspiring book *Big Magic*, acclaimed writer Elizabeth Gilbert asks: "Do you have the courage to bring forth the treasures that are hidden within you?"[30] She continues "[S]urely something wonderful is sheltered inside you. I say this with all confidence, because I happen to believe that we are all walking repositories of buried treasure. I believe this is one of the oldest and most generous tricks the universe plays on us human beings, both for its own amusement and for ours: The universe buries strange jewels deep within us all, and then stands back to see if we can find them. The hunt to uncover those jewels—that's creative living."[31] While I hope her words move you as they did me, note that I am not suggesting that leaning into your creativity requires that you quit your full-time job in order to become an artist. No, this chapter is merely a nudge toward inviting more imagination and whimsy into your life, weaving them together with the pragmatism of daily life as a lawyer.

I see hobbies as a lost art form. I remember talking to a partner nearing retirement and I asked him how he managed to maintain such a long career in a stressful BigLaw environment. Without blinking, he responded: "The law is a jealous mistress, so you have to let her know from the beginning that you're not in a monogamous relationship." After recovering from a fit of uncomfortable laughter over the slightly inappropriate analogy, I probed him to elaborate. He said that, like most male lawyers when he started out, he got married during law school and had children starting in his first year of practice. Although life was less complicated then—no computers, no cellphones, no clients across state lines, ahh sounds like a dream!—he and his wife were committed to each having a life outside of the home. For him, that meant playing chess every week and collecting wartime memorabilia. While his hobbies ebbed and flowed over the years, one thing remained the same: his commitment to setting a time every week to do something "just for the hell of it." When he looked back on his career, he had countless proud moments of winning trials and closing large clients. No such accolades accompanied his hobbies and yet, he told me that he learned just as much from a friendly game of chess as he did from attending a well-known trial college. He and Gilbert would agree that creativity feeds our soul in a way that no other pursuit can. His goal was never to become a chess champion or to start a side hustle or even to be recognized in any of his endeavors; rather, it was purely an activity for the sake of doing something unrelated to the law or his family obligations.

This was such an important lesson for me to hear early on in my career because the truth is, we all need a reprieve from this tasking job. If you don't learn to intentionally fill your time with a hobby you want to pursue, you will simply revert to work mode. We all dream of having more time to do things that make us happy, but if we did gain a few extra hours a day, what would we actually do with them? Clean the house, catch up on work, scroll through our phones, maybe call a friend, or spend more time with our families. Humans aren't great at allocating free time. And this is why we can thank other humans for having created a magical tool called the calendar. Yes, the calendar is unsexy and doesn't quite scream creativity, but for the sake of starting and sticking with a hobby, there is no better device. We are far more likely to devote time to an activity if we can find a place for it in our calendars and make it an appointment.

Cultivating Worthwhile Hobbies

The best way I've found to cultivate hobbies is to combine a habit with a hobby and turn them into a "habby." I just made up this term, so I'm pretty sure it won't end up in a dictionary anytime soon. But stick with me here. Nearly every hobby out there requires some form of consistency in order to truly reap the benefits. If you love reading, but only read a book every blue moon, you are actually less likely to increase how frequently you read unless you begin associating reading with something you already do. For instance, do you lie in bed scrolling your phone every night? *Everyone raises hand*. Okay, you already lie in bed nightly without actually falling asleep. Why not keep a book on your nightstand? I can't guarantee that you will throw your phone out in favor of a book, but you will actually pick up that book more than once. Do you like having an afternoon coffee while scrolling the internets as a break? Why not place a book by your laptop so that at least a couple of times a week, you'll choose the book over the siren song of online news?

I tell everyone I know that my dog is my hobby, or rather my "habby." That might sound odd, but if you think about it, having a dog requires that you get into the habit of walking him/her, feeding him/her, playing, etc., while also providing you with tremendous entertainment and something that you hopefully enjoy doing or else you wouldn't have gotten a dog. I cherish my early morning walks with my dog—they are both a habit and a hobby. I love the quiet before most of my neighbors wake up, and sometimes we see a family of raccoons hoisting up a tree or a dreaded cat, which sends my dog into a frenzy. The walks are always the same, but somehow also different. This is not only my dog's time to sniff out what went down in the neighborhood the night before, but also my time to think, mentally plan out my day, and resolve unresolved thoughts from the previous night. It's only 15 minutes of my day (once my dog has done his rounds, he basically sprints home for breakfast), but it's easily one of my most creative periods. I let my thoughts go where they want to go, without an agenda, and I can't tell you how frequently I've come home from this walk with a new viewpoint that I hadn't considered before or with a remarkably straightforward solution to an issue I kept having. Dogs are a remarkable habby!

If you are in the market for a new habby, I suggest first looking at routines you already have and seeing where you might be able to fit something fun in. Don't make this hard on yourself. Below are some ideas to get your creative juices flowing:

- Something to make: art, crafts, crocheting, knitting, home décor, pottery;

- Something to think: reading, puzzles, word games, chess, trivia;

- Something to feel: volunteering for a cause near to your heart, getting involved with faith-based organizations, helping at-risk kids with reading comprehension, fostering pets;

- Something to move: yoga, biking, swimming, walking your dog, group fitness classes, dance, barre classes.

Another hobby that took me much longer to cultivate is yoga. I have been practicing yoga since high school—before the days of Instagram yoga influencers and beautifully appointed yoga studios. As a two-sport athlete in high school, my body was constantly sore and beat up. A friend of mine whose parents are actual hippies recommended that we try a yoga class with a 60-something-year-old instructor who could put her legs behind her head like a pretzel. I was immediately hooked—not because of the human pretzel—but because of the vacillation between calm and intensity I experienced during my first class. Yoga offers the unique combination of meditative peace and resolute power through its flow from pose to pose.

I have been practicing yoga for over 20 years now. While still working as a lawyer, I decided I wanted to get certified to teach yoga. For those of you who think getting this certification simply means showing up for a few classes and taking a quick test, you are seriously underestimating the gatekeeping surrounding this 5,000-year-old practice. The governing body for yoga practitioners in the United States requires a minimum of 200 hours of directed yoga practice, plus a crap-ton of study material, all culminating in a final written exam *and* a live showcase. It's no joke. So I decided I wanted to do it. After all, us lawyers love nothing more than a good certificate, right?

I enrolled at my local yoga studio and dutifully put my training schedule directly into my work calendar: classes would take place every Tuesday and Thursday from 5:00 to 7:00 pm, plus a few weekend-long intensives sprinkled throughout. I told everyone at work about this commitment and made clear that I would not miss a single class because near-perfect attendance is a prerequisite for the certificate. Again, these yogis don't mess around! What happened next was completely unexpected: while my colleagues and partners respected my schedule and didn't push back on my boundary, I tried to fit in a full working day into the days I had to leave early for my yoga classes, leaving me depleted and fatigued. I would make it to the class, but my head would be spinning with unfinished projects, running to-do lists, and guilt for not being able to accomplish my work faster. This was a crucial lesson for me: making the time on a calendar is not sufficient when you are adding something but don't subtract something else. It's not just about the time commitment, there is also an energy component: how can you engage in an activity wholly if you are still carrying the burden of a full workload?

Of course, the solution here isn't to quit your job so that you can have a hobby. That would be a ridiculous suggestion. However, based on all the research I included on the importance of creativity and joy in our lives, I do urge you to practice making time in your schedule for a hobby. I do not recommend trying to pack all of your commitments in a shorter timeframe, crossing your fingers that you will somehow be able to get it all done. It doesn't work. Being intentional about developing a hobby has the added bonus of commitment: if you dedicate allotted time in your schedule for this activity *and* you get rid of something else, you have just set yourself up for long-term involvement with this hobby.

I did eventually obtain my yoga teacher certificate, but it came years later after I left the law and embarked on my current profession in attorney development. It turns out that taking a job I loved afforded me much more energy to take on other passion projects, like the yoga teacher training, writing my first book, starting my coaching business, and now writing this book. We make lots of assumptions about the equation of time—it's not just numerical time that impacts our ability to accomplish things, but also time in the form of energy. The question then isn't how much time do you have, but how much energy for each given activity?

I love yoga for many reasons: not only for the physical gains of moving your body, stretching, and building flexibility, but also for the mental benefits of focus, meditation, and clear-headedness. Yoga taught me an important lesson that I believe translates well to the practice of law: perfect doesn't exist. You never perfect a yoga pose or a sequence. Even the most experienced yoga practitioners know that the goal of yoga is continued practice. Results are never guaranteed—in yoga, in life, or in a career. Practicing law is similar. Its gift lies in the never-ending learning opportunities and the continuous growth as a lawyer. Even the most brilliant legal minds will admit that they do not know everything. And why would they want to? Our lives—both personal and professional—are only enhanced by the lessons life teaches us. Not to get overly morbid in a chapter about hobbies, but I believe that the end of learning is the end of life.

Friendships Feed the Soul

While networking is a buzzword in the legal industry, how many lawyers do you call your real friends? Even better, how many non-lawyers do you regularly socialize with? My circle skewed pretty lawyer-heavy with the exception of a few close friends from high school and college until I made it a mission to expand it to a very particular ensemble: former lawyers who have abandoned the law for other careers. I mostly took this on as a personal inquiry into what fascinating lives former lawyers lead, but it became much more than that. I believe friendships require a certain level of vulnerability—you have to share a little piece of your insecurities with the other person, then that person does the same with you, and this mutual act forges a connection. As I never quite felt like I belonged in the legal profession, my offering to the former lawyers I sought out as friends was a simple but genuine "I see you." The conversations started out a bit awkward, contrived small talk while getting to know each other, then eventually evolved into hour-long video meetings where we exchanged ideas about reimagining the field of law, building stronger communities of former lawyers, and revealing where we feel the most self-doubt and impostor syndrome.

Where did I find all these new friends? LinkedIn. Seriously. I could give an entire masterclass on how to use the platform to not only network for professional purposes, but also to build a personal brand or launch a business. The secrets: (1) post regularly, (2) add contacts and engage with their content, and (3) speak authentically. Gone are the days of LinkedIn being a place to humblebrag about getting a promotion or winning some lawyer award; the most popular posts now reflect the human side of work. People talk about pay disparity, pregnancy discrimination, mental health struggles, lack of diversity in law firms, harassment, judicial overreach, war, job loss, and everything in between. I had fewer than 900 followers on LinkedIn when I decided to start posting three days a week and curate my content to attract a specific audience. Within six months of pursuing this strategy, I gained 1,600 new followers. These were folks who repeatedly commented on my posts, referred clients, or became clients themselves, and opened new doors for me in a variety of industries. I ended up giving paid speeches, group trainings, and quite a few podcast interviews. None of it—and I cannot emphasize this point enough—would have taken place if I hadn't created a blueprint for showing up on the platform as myself, talking about topics I care about, and realizing that not everyone will like or agree with me.

If you read the above paragraph and thought to yourself, "Yeah, okay, my firm definitely doesn't want me being authentic on social media," you're likely correct. I won't argue with you there. While some firms have embraced and even encouraged their attorneys to build their online presence, most are stuck in medieval times and still cling to the antique belief that a lawyer is a suit without personality. Here's where I would push back (on you, not the firm): So what? If you post about something that you genuinely care about, that doesn't offend a bunch of people, and isn't a call to overthrow the government, what harm does that cause to your firm? And if your firm takes issue with that, then what kind of BS do they stand for? Is this a place where you'd really want to build your career and your reputation? If the alternative to posting is to stay silent and pretend you're someone else, then what a huge exertion of energy on your part! Again, for what? So that the firm partners give you a pat on the back and acknowledge you for being another suit *just* like them? Trying to mold yourself into a set of expectations that you don't personally value is going to send you into an existential crisis sooner rather than later. So I'm here to gently persuade you that:

Being punished for authenticity in the long run will serve
you much better than being rewarded for conformity

One of my most cherished friendships from this LinkedIn
experiment is a woman I will call Serena. A single mother, she left
a financially successful law firm partnership in order to build a
dog daycare center for senior dogs. Though we bonded over our
obvious love of dogs, our similarities pretty much end there. We
grew up in vastly different families, live on opposite coasts, I am
happily childfree, she's a Virgo, the list goes on. Yet we both made
the conscious decision that we would nurture this friendship and
make both the time and space for each other even when (especially
when) things got hectic. What has kept us going strong for years is
not just the frequency of our communications, but the depth. We are
honest about our struggles, our hopes, our impossible pipedreams.
She was the first person I told I wanted to write a book and she
often reminds me that owning a business catered to doggos isn't
the walk in the park I make it out to be in my head. Yes, we give
each other business advice, but we're also intimately familiar with
the other's personal life. In the beginning, we spent a lot of time
philosophizing about why we left the law and how it's an inherently
difficult profession because that's what we had in common. Our
friendship has expanded beyond that now and I'm happy to say we
rarely bring up our old demons.

The point of this illustration is that while it is insanely helpful
to make friends with folks who have been in the trenches with you,
true growth comes from the ability to move forward and build a
new future together with these friends. I still have a ton of friends
who practice law. To some extent, I have less in common with them
today than I did when I was still practicing, but I still feel a close
bond due to our shared experiences. So I invite you to widen your
circle because you will be much better for it.

III

Create Your Chill

A. Choosing Your Career Vision

After my decade of practicing law and several years coaching lawyers, I have met hundreds of lawyers who have created careers they love. Unfortunately, law schools do not spend nearly enough time and resources getting their students to think intentionally about how to build a sustaining career. They mostly shuffle law students around from government to firm to in-house roles without putting much emphasis on a curated career.

What is a curated career? It's one that involves deep reflection, intentional thought, and a vastly different set of questions than we currently ask ourselves in law school about how to choose a path. It also requires lots and lots of discussions with other lawyers and legal professionals about their jobs. It is nearly impossible to research every potential legal job out there before deciding which to embark on, but getting real-life accounts from people in those jobs is unmatched. When I was considering leaving the law to pursue another career, I spent hours conducting informational interviews. Yes, they are awkward, time-consuming, and sometimes met with rejection. But more often than not, lawyers are extremely generous with their time and love talking about their career paths. (If you haven't yet realized this, lawyers are obsessed with work.)

So in this chapter, I endeavor to create a blueprint for curating a career. This is based on my own experiments in my career and the numerous discussions I've had with lawyers and my coaching clients. This is not the gospel or the end-all to all of your career woes, however, because job satisfaction and purpose are tenets that we all struggle with at different points in our lives. As I have pivoted from law firm to in-house back to law firm and eventually to a non-practicing role, you might also find yourself pivoting several times throughout a (hopefully) long career. As they say, you can do anything with a law degree! It might be a cliché, but I have found it to be a completely accurate one.

Step 1 – Likes/dislikes/tolerates

You might be sick of reading about likes, dislikes, and tolerates by now, but it is the most important initial step in carving out a satisfying and fulfilling career. There is no way around this step because this is what curating a career is all about: taking into account your individual attributes and matching them to jobs that can support you and your family financially. Most of us do it the other way: we take a job based on mostly external factors, and then we try to contort ourselves to fit that job description. We set aside our intuition, our gut feeling that something is off; instead, we march forward and convince ourselves that it feels hard because it's worth it. But here's the thing: there is a difference between a challenging job and a difficult job. The former has flavors of excitement, upskilling, and rewards for the hard parts; the latter leaves you feeling defeated, inauthentic, and unable to succeed. Usually a difficult job just isn't the right job for you.

When creating your likes/dislikes/tolerates list, I want you to consider:

When do you like yourself the most?

We all get these glimpses of joy, enthusiasm, giddiness over solving a puzzle, creativity, flow, pride, and feel-good moments throughout the day. These moments often go unnoticed, but if you stop to pinpoint exactly what is happening, you might say something like "I wish I could do this all day" or "I would do this for free." Instead of waiting around for something like this to take place organically (because, let's face it, it might take a while for you to observe!), you could journal when you like yourself the most. If you find it difficult to answer this question, pretend that someone is going to videotape you at work to put it on YouTube and of course, you want to show your best side. So is it when you are solving a complex problem? Is it when you are working in a team? Or when you are presenting an argument to a group? Or when you are explaining to a client the roadmap for her case? What are the parts of your day or your current job that truly make you feel authentic?

If this exercise becomes frustrating to you, another option is to ask a trusted friend or family member what he or she believes is the best version of you. Sometimes we are surprised by what others so easily see as our best attributes. For instance, a friend of mine told me that I was like a Sherpa for our group of lawyer friends, wisely guiding them through difficult decisions in their careers. She said that this ability to help our friends reflect on how they were doing certain things at work or why they were engaging in catastrophizing behaviors appeared to come naturally to me. And she was right! I get a huge amount of satisfaction from helping lawyers navigate their careers. But don't get me wrong: I am not always a sympathetic shoulder to cry on or someone who will listen for hours on end to a problem. I am solution-driven and action-oriented by nature, so my gift lies in encouraging lawyers to make a decision that serves them better than the current situation they are in. I don't tolerate indecisiveness or complaining without a plan of action. As you might imagine, sometimes my friends just need someone to listen and empathize, which isn't always my best suit.

It's important to get granular when answering the question of when you like yourself the most because there are many facets to every answer. You might excel in a certain aspect of an activity, but not in all aspects of it. Simply saying "I like myself best when I am negotiating a case settlement" doesn't take into account the type of case, who is on the other end of that negotiation, who is your client, the setting of this negotiation, and so on. These statements contain a lot of nuance you should be digging through in order to find the truest version for you.

The phrases you come up during this exercise translate well into your "likes" list. Think of this list as an opportunity to create your ideal job description. If you were the architect of a job that reflected 100% the work you wanted to do, what would it look like? Don't worry about how realistic it is right now. The question you are trying to answer is how would you like to fill your workday? If you remove the barriers of practicality, you will start to see common themes show up in your list. For instance, you might learn that you seek out innovation, or that you thrive in an environment with clearly delineated rules and duties, or that you enjoy working alone more than with others. All of these seemingly fragmented likes actually reflect pieces of who you are that, when viewed together, form the basis of your work persona.

When it comes to dislikes, it's easy to just write down the opposite of your likes. After all, if I like something, then I must dislike the opposite, right? Well, that's partly true, but we're lawyers, so let's get a little more detailed. Your dislikes should represent work tasks that are absolutely insufferable to you. I want you to ask yourself: "If I were being punished, what type of work would I be given?" These are tasks that fill you with dread, boredom, fear, anxiety, heart palpitations, the works. You should not be ambiguous or tolerant when describing your dislikes. The point isn't to simply list items on the other side of the spectrum of your likes, but rather to come up with serious encroachments of when you feel at your best.

Sometimes a dislike is disguised as something you're actually good at and have been rewarded for in the past. These can be sneaky dislikes because we've been running on autopilot, performing for the reward even though we actively detest doing the task. To give you an example, I am an outstanding and some might say tough negotiator. When I worked in-house, I took over settlement negotiations in several cases because I didn't think our outside counsel represented the company's interests well and I wound up settling these cases for significantly below what our attorneys had estimated. Given my litigation background, I excel at finding holes in the other side's case and can usually convince them to reduce their demand. Even though I am proficient and have been praised for this quality, I absolutely hate doing it. I hate the gamesmanship, the pretense, waiting for the other person to blink first. The whole thing gives me hives and I just want it to end, thank you very much. A job where I am expected to negotiate frequently would be a horrible fit for me. It took me years to uncover this hidden dislike but it is now very high at the top of my list.

Not all of your dislikes have to be "serious." For instance, after many years in litigation, one of my absolute dislikes is business wear. It sounds silly, but I cannot and will not be forced to wear suits or heels or any kind of courtroom attire. Several years ago, when I was still practicing law, I got a new firm headshot taken. I was wearing a boring black suit jacket in my previous headshot and I wanted to update it to reflect my personality a bit more. So I put on a chunky necklace I loved and a black top (yes, still black, but no suit jacket!). After my picture was posted on the firm website, a colleague decided that it was a great opportunity to give her opinion and she told me that my headshot was "kind of unprofessional." I was so taken aback that I didn't even ask her what she meant by that. Looking back on that moment, I realize that I didn't really care what she meant. Her (rude) statement was a rejection of my personality, a reminder that I didn't belong in that firm. I don't necessarily fault her for pointing this out to me—in some ways, she was right. It helped me realize that looking professional (whatever that means) is not a metric on which I wish to be evaluated. If the standard in a job is dressing in court-appropriate clothing, then I am not a good fit. Of course, this isn't just about workwear—the bigger theme here is authenticity.

As you complete your list of dislikes, you will see, as you did with your list of likes, that a common theme emerges. It isn't simply about what your dislikes mean at their face value, but what deeper signals do they convey? So many of us want to push these dislikes to the side and tell ourselves that we can muddle through. We take our parents' idioms—it's called work, not fun—to heart and we believe that unpleasantness is part of the job. Don't get me wrong, all jobs have a level of tribulation, but you should not be experiencing more dislikes than likes on a daily basis. The equilibrium found in a career that actually suits your individual needs always skews in favor of likes. You are allowed to feel like yourself at work, not like an impostor impersonating the lawyer you are expected to be at the office.

In some ways, putting together your list of tolerates is a bit less tasking. Here, you are simply outlining work that you don't love, you don't hate, but you don't want to be doing frequently. Another way of looking at this list is: What do you feel so-so about? As an example, I give a fair amount of presentations both at work and in my coaching practice, and a necessary part of that is creating PowerPoint presentations. This is something I can tolerate. I wouldn't say it's my favorite thing to do, but I really don't mind it. I often work out a template that I then recycle for other presentations, so it makes it less painful than starting from scratch. Over the years, I have learned to put the bare minimum amount of work into the slides so that it frees me creatively to think through a solid presentation. You might find similar aspects of your work—these are tasks that support your likes but you don't enjoy them enough to make your list of likes. Every job will have its own tolerates. The secret is to keep them from occurring so frequently that they turn into dislikes.

Likes

Dislikes

Tolerates

Once you have compiled your lists, the final step here is to pull out a few running themes. If you have done the work with sufficient introspection and detail, these themes will jump out at you relatively quickly. If you struggle with this, ask a friend or trusted co-worker to read them out loud to you. Not only will your friend be able to help you figure this out, but you'll get a better sense too from hearing someone else state your likes, dislikes, and tolerates.

Step 2 – How is your current job serving you?

If you are currently in a job that fails to satisfy you on multiple levels, it may appear impossible to find a single aspect that you enjoy. I've been there. Here's the thing: when we are unhappy at work, we often lump everything related to this job together and call it all bad. Because we are so deflated, it's nearly impossible to pinpoint specifically what it is we dislike about our role and, more importantly, what drew us to this job in the first place.

I coached a client who had spent nearly a decade in a practice area at three different law firms. To say that she had enough was an understatement. The first words out of her mouth during our initial coaching call were: "If I don't find a completely new career within a year, I am afraid that I will have a mental breakdown at work, quit, and move to Greece—with or without my husband!" In no uncertain terms, she was completely burned out and divorced from her chosen path. When I assigned her the exercise of exploring what she liked in her job, I thought she was going to jump through the computer screen and rip my eyes out. Thankfully, she did not and went on to complete the exercise as dutifully as most lawyers do. But here's the kicker: she actually wound up listing seven different aspects of her practice area that she really enjoyed. And she didn't waffle when choosing these items either; she stressed that these were skills that she had worked hard to build and that she enjoyed every opportunity to apply them at work. More than that, she told me that she wanted to find ways to continue implementing some of these responsibilities in her new career.

The point here isn't that if you undertake this exercise, you will magically learn to love your job. But there is something to honor in the job that made you excited at one time. Why did you apply in the first place? Was it the people, the substantive work, the name recognition, the potential for advancement? Whatever your reasons were, can you try to unearth them and see if they still hold true? Alternatively, have you discovered new aspects of your job that you enjoy? Have you learned anything about yourself in this position that you didn't know before?

One aspect of your job that might be working for you is money. It's okay to admit that. While many of us were taught that it's rude to discuss finances, it's easily one of the biggest stressors of adult life. There is a running joke about getting into the law to help people and staying for the money, but let's face it, the compensation certainly helps. While this book is mainly focused on helping lawyers create a happy and fulfilling life in and out of the law, I would be remiss if I didn't include a discussion about the financial opportunities available in this profession. According to the U.S. Bureau of Labor Statistics, the mean annual wage for lawyers as of May 2023 was $176,470.[32] In the top paying states for lawyers, like New York and California, those annual mean wages exceeded $200,000.[33] If you are a first-generation college student or the primary provider for your family, it's hard to cast these numbers aside in pursuit of the elusive work-life balance.

There is a place for "and" here: you can acknowledge that you're in it for the money *and* that you have the ability to redesign your career in a way that fits you better. While you may not have the financial freedom (yet) to throw it all away and start a coffee shop that serves only lavender lattes, you can assess what works in your job now and what you might be able to experiment with so that you tilt the balance between an unbearable situation and one that you can live with. The first step to achieving that is examining what you like about your current role. Then, after some reflection, start thinking about how you could do more of what you like and delegate the things you don't love. A misfit job doesn't always have to be a zero-sum game. If you take a look at your career from a different angle, you might learn that there are ways to make it work for you without affecting your bank account.

Ways in which my current job serves me

Step 3 – Strengths and Not-So-Strengths

Dr. Don Clifton (the creator of the CliftonStrengths® assessment) is famous for saying that people's weaknesses will never develop but that their strengths will develop infinitely. The law is a critical profession; we thrive on poking holes in others' arguments, endlessly perfecting work product, and spotting mistakes in written documents. I am not sure who invented the redline feature in Word, but I'd venture a guess it's used by lawyers more than any other professional. No wonder there is an undercurrent of inadequacy and impostor syndrome among lawyers. As much as we try to develop a thick skin in the face of constant criticism, it's hard to keep it up.

Here's my sell: let's say you are an average writer but you excel at negotiating case settlements. The tendency for most lawyers is to keep improving their writing skills, while relying on their mostly natural talent in negotiations. It sort of makes sense—why focus on something you're already good at instead of trying to get better at something you're not good at? But what if I told you that, even if you put in all the effort in the world to become a better writer, you would at most increase your capacity from an average writer to an above-average writer. Where does that put you in the legal profession, where you may very well be surrounded by a number of excellent writers? You're still in the middle of the pack. On the other hand, if you could go from a great negotiator to potentially one of the best negotiators at your firm, well, now you're a rockstar. This is what Don Clifton is getting at: it's infinitely harder to scale up your weaknesses to the point that they actually turn into strengths, while it is much easier to make even marginal improvements on your strengths and turn them into superpowers.

Personally I like to refer to weakness as "not-so-strengths." Why? Because I don't believe in assigning a negative meaning to attributes we have that (1) we can't really eliminate, and (2) it makes no sense to try to force ourselves to keep cultivating. Our not-so-strengths aren't meant to be feared, hidden, or shamed into perfection. They just are. They exist with us. Naming them won't make them take over your life and overpower your strengths. Accepting that you're not really great at something won't make you a lesser lawyer or somehow undermine your ability to succeed. Quite the opposite: the ability to see the parts of you that aren't as strong as others gives you a clarity and self-awareness that few people possess. It allows you to move through this world in a way that is authentic and prone to less friction because you know what you excel at and where you need to ask for help.

When identifying your strengths and not-so-strengths, I think of them as two sides of the same coin: the opposite of your strength is very often your not-so-strength. For example, one of my strengths is that I am action-oriented. The way this plays out in my life is that I am quick to make decisions, create a course of action, and follow it through. I don't dawdle or get paralyzed by indecision. When life doesn't work out as planned (as it has a tendency to do every once in a while), I can pivot and set on a new course without getting bogged down in the mind drama of things not going exactly the way I wanted them to. As you are reading this description of one of my strengths, I bet you can already get a sense of my not-so-strength: thoughtfulness. In my eagerness to act quickly and make a decision, I sometimes don't take the time to weigh all my options and truly assess the situation as a whole. While I've mostly benefitted from playing up my strength, there have been times when I should have acted more carefully.

Even though I realize this about myself, am I all of the sudden going to change my whole persona and become the most thoughtful, tactical decision-maker ever? Nah. Again, the purpose of this exercise is not to assess your not-so-strengths in order to transform them into superpowers; rather, it's an endeavor to better verbalize what makes you who you are. If you are struggling with coming up with strengths and their opposites, I suggest asking your parents, siblings, or partner. And don't be offended if any of these individuals are able to rattle off your attributes faster than you can "chill." Sometimes people know us better than we know ourselves.

Another way to determine your strengths is by taking an online assessment. I am partial to the StrengthsFinder[34] I mentioned earlier because it was the only tool that not only lists your top strengths, but also offers a detailed report of how these strengths manifest at work and how they motivate you. For instance, my top strength—strategic— puts me in the roles of thinker, evaluator, pathfinder, and makes me willing to consider possibilities that others don't see. The values I bring to the workplace include creative anticipation, persistence, and imagination. My demotivator is someone telling me we need to take a certain action because that's the way it's always been done. These descriptors accompany all of my top strengths in the report, which offer a rich vocabulary to express my needs and wants in a job. Even though learning my strengths wasn't a surprise, the way they interact with one another to build up my entire personality is fascinating.

List your strengths and not-so-strengths below, and watch the magic unfold:

Strengths	**Not-so-strengths**

Step 4 – Vision Statement

Okay, you've completed your list of likes/dislikes/tolerates, you recounted the ways in which your current job works for you, and you've identified your strengths and not-so-strengths. Now it's time to get weird and draft your vision statement. No, it's not one of those arts and crafts activities where you cut out magazine pages that say "Your dream is just one wish away!" and plaster them on a poster as a way to manifest your dream job. We're lawyers, so instead of pictures, let's use our words.

This step involves crafting a short statement of your ideal week in your ideal job, written in the present tense as if you are already living it. Here, you are actually putting into words what your life would look like if you worked in a role you loved. It's the reverse of job searching: instead of trying to fit into a job description, you're writing it yourself. The reason this exercise works is because it allows you to combine aspirational desires with realistic demands to see what might be possible. From this vision statement you can then work backwards to find positions that resemble your intention. You might not be able to find an exact match, but if you can't even verbalize what you want, how will you know when you find it?

This exercise is one of the toughest for my clients to complete, so I offer a few examples. While you needn't follow a specific template, your vision statement will be much stronger if it includes these details: (1) typical working hours, (2) level of interaction with co-workers, clients, and others, (3) detailed description of substantive job duties (building on your likes/dislikes/tolerates list), (4) attributes valued in this role (weaving in your strengths and not-so-strengths), and (5) future opportunities in this position. You want to be illustrative and precise so that it feels like a genuine job description.

Karla's Vision Statement

I am a partner at a small law firm I started with a law school classmate. We handle estate planning, probate litigation and a few family law matters our clients refer to us. While our standard office hours are 9:00 am to 4:00 pm, I like to get started on my day before my kids wake up by planning out my appointments and checking in with my law partner on our top priorities. I am then able to do the morning routine with the kids, and I don't show up at the office frazzled and unprepared. I meet with clients both in person and virtually, which I do nearly daily because my favorite part of my job is interacting with them. Since administrative duties are my not-so-strength, I rely heavily on two assistants. We schedule meetings a few times during the day to ensure we are on the same page, but not constantly interrupt each other's work.

Every Friday my law partner and I have coffee outside of the office and discuss our law firm strategy. While we both agree that we could bring on another lawyer, our goal for the firm is not expansion, but rather deepening our expertise and up-leveling our client base. We are also intentional about creating an excellent place to work for our assistants so that they can build long-term careers with us.

Allan's Vision Statement

I work in-house as commercial counsel for a large tech company. While my practice area is niche, I am often asked to pitch in for my colleagues and thus constantly learn new aspects of our business. I eventually want to report to our company's Chief Legal Officer, so I am taking every opportunity I can to expand my knowledge. While this means I sometimes work outside my general 9:00 am to 6:00 pm schedule, I do it out of genuine interest. Another favorite part of my job is traveling to our company's campuses around the country and abroad as I assist with high-value commercial deals.

Getting to know colleagues around the world is integral not only to my current role, but also to my future promotion. I am also an avid traveler myself, so this aspect of the job suits me well.

I struggle with my attention span, which sometimes poses issues when I have a detail-oriented project, but I have learned to double- and triple-check my work in order to avoid big errors. The fact that I am constantly working on new projects is ideal for my not-so-strength. I know that as I move up in the organization, my attention deficit might become a challenge, so I am working on advocating for an assistant to help me in that department. Regardless, I am confident that my dedication to this company and ability to work well across many business units will take me in the right direction.

Kim's Vision Statement

I run a growing fitness studio offering a mix of yoga, Pilates and barre classes. While our studio is open seven days a week, I only teach classes from 9:00 am to noon. After I finish teaching, I do general administrative work for the studio, which encompasses everything from social media marketing, responding to studio client inquiries, setting up workshops and special events, dealing with our vendors, and managing several part-time teachers. My favorite part of owning this studio is that I get to use my legal education in several ways, but my relationship with work is much less intense and formal, and way more fun than when I was practicing law. My job is to create a peaceful and welcoming environment for our clients so that they can destress from their jobs.

In some ways, my work never stops because our studio doesn't run in a traditional workweek fashion. Yet I feel energized and motivated to keep growing our brand because I believe it truly helps people. Fitness has also changed my life, so working in it doesn't feel like actual work. My goal is to open a second studio and possibly work with a partner to run the second location. The more we can grow our current client base and our rainy-day funds, the more likely this goal is to come true.

I also realize that my not-so-strength lies in the finance aspect of running a business. While I am not a spender by any means, I am quite sloppy when it comes to using the studio's money wisely. To that end, I am in the process of outsourcing the bookkeeping to a professional so that I can focus on what I love to do.

Once written, your vision statement should serve as the springboard for creating a strategy to either take your current job to the next level or build skills to help you move on to the next phase in your career. If you've learned nothing else from this book, I hope you take away the idea that

planning + action = dreams come true

Both are necessary ingredients to building a life you love. Planning without action is just daydreaming, while action without planning is how nightmares come true. For folks who sometimes blindly enter a three-year law school commitment without a whole lot of thought into what a career might look like post-graduation, lawyers can be reluctant to attempt to design their careers. But I'd like to remind you that we are the same folks who die at our desks, ignore our kids until it's too late, succumb to the demands of our legal careers, drink too much, and generally numb ourselves to the beatdown from our chosen profession. Yes, it may be uncomfortable to sit down and work on yourself, but the alternative is much grimmer.

Step 5 – Current experiments and skill-building

This step is where we put our plans to the test. Here I offer two suggestions and it's reader's choice whether you want to implement both or just one. The first suggestion is to conduct small experiments in your current job that align more with the type of work you envision doing to see if you actually enjoy it. How many times have you heard of a job that sounds great only to stop and ask yourself, how will I know if I like it? And truly, how could you know? It's one thing to have had a college internship at a company that you liked and imagine what it might be like to work there now; it's a completely different experience to just try a job without any prior exposure whatsoever. Here is where an experiment in your current position might prove to be a risk-free option. For instance, say you're interested in a career in marketing but all you've ever done is practice law. How could you experiment with marketing-related work?

- If you firm already has a marketing department, you could reach out to the leader and offer to help on some discrete tasks.

- If you work at a smaller firm, you could start by creating a marketing strategy for your practice or even for the entire firm and see if the firm would let you run with it.

- You could offer to help an entrepreneurial friend with marketing ideas for her business (maybe even do it for free to get the experience).

- You could write an article or a series of articles and learn how to market them on social media or for publication.

- If you are involved with a nonprofit or a local organization, you could volunteer to run the next marketing campaign (I promise any organization will love you for this!).

This example can be translated across numerous job ideas. There are countless ways in which you could experiment in a non-committed way with a potential career avenue before jumping in. Does it require some extra time? Yes, but the upside is huge. You will either discover that you are really interested and skilled in this budding career interest (yay!) or that you hate it and would never want to take it on as a full-time gig (which is good to know before quitting your job). One question that might come up for you is whether or not to share this with your boss. On one hand, it might be taken as a sign that you're ready to bounce (which could very well be the truth!); on the other, you might be surprised to learn that your current employer is willing to let you experiment.

The latter was actually my own experience when I became interested in law firm administration. I was working as a litigation attorney when the pandemic hit. I had a case set for trial in March 2020 and as soon as it became apparent that the pandemic would last longer than a few weeks, all of my trial-set cases for the foreseeable future were paused. Courts closed and our clients frantically sent "stop work" emails to everyone at our firm. It was rough for my billable hours, but a blessing in disguise for my idea to experiment with working in firm administration. After talking to a friend who had successfully transitioned from practicing law to attorney development within the same firm, I decided to shoot my shot. So one day I reached out to our firm's Chief Operating Officer and expressed my interest in learning more about the back office operations of the firm. I was incredibly nervous and knew I was risking him relaying my email to other firm leaders, which could lead to questions about my commitment to my law practice.

To my absolute delight, he responded that the firm had been wanting to explore an emerging practice area, but none of the lawyers had the bandwidth to learn this area and become proficient enough to market it to clients. He said that my email caught him at the right time as he was preparing to tell our Firm Managing Partner that we needed to drop the idea. I had never heard of this area of the law, but as he explained to me, building up this new practice would require working with internal stakeholders at the firm, such as our Chief Marketing Officer, Chief Diversity Officer, Accounting, and the firm's Executive Committee. While only a small part was actually related to firm administration, this experiment gave me the opportunity to see firsthand what all these different departments did. If you've only practiced law at a law firm, you might have a vague idea of how the firm is run, but you wouldn't know all the ins and outs. I loved getting a behind-the-scenes look at how these departments support the firm's clients in ways other than actively working on their cases. I also learned that politics don't stop just because you're not practicing law. This experiment lasted less than a year because both the firm and I realized that we would have many hurdles to clear with our current clients before launching this practice. I had never anticipated all the intricacies involved in setting up a new group and the many conflicts (both within the firm and externally) that require attention when entering uncharted territory.

Though the experiment was short-lived and ultimately did not become my next career, it absolutely laid the foundation for my transition into attorney development and legal recruiting, and eventually my coaching business. It allowed me to think outside of the lawyer box and I got to actually work in law firm administration without taking on a new job. It was weirdly similar to an internship, but one where I still get paid a lot of money. I am forever grateful to my old firm for trusting me to try something new. At the end of the day, only you can gauge whether or not your employer would be equally responsive to offering you a similar experiment. Like the old saying goes, "If you don't ask, the answer will always be no."

The second suggestion is to identify what additional skills you would need if you were to pursue a different career, and which exercise you could implement in tandem with the experiments. Going back to the marketing example, if you take up one or two experiments and realize that you really enjoy working in marketing but that there are certain proficiencies you lack, this would be the perfect time to invest in a course or a coaching program that would help solidify your qualifications for a new role. Many lawyers I've met (myself included) are eager to continue their education and amass certifications, so this suggestion shouldn't be a hard sell.

However, I do want to stress that it's crucial that you first pinpoint what it is you are trying to achieve as opposed to enrolling in a program simply because you excel in school. The goal here is to get you closer to that dream career, not to hop in and out of interesting-sounding classes just for fun.[35] If you do decide that additional courses would be required, be mindful of the never-ending preparation stage that often paralyzes lawyers from taking action. It's fine to enroll in classes, but *studying for* something is not the same as *doing* the actual thing. At some point, you have to move from the research phase to the work phase.

Also keep in mind that not all job changes require you to obtain new skills. Truly, most legal experiences translate well to other fields. I've coached quite a few lawyers who were stuck in their beliefs that once a lawyer, always a lawyer. They did not understand that there is truth underneath the saying "You can do anything with a law degree." But show me a job—any job—where written and verbal communication, responsiveness, client service, attention to detail, ability to translate difficult concepts into practical advice, and critical thinking aren't valued. Remove the legalese and the courts, and lawyers essentially work in sales, customer service, consulting, people management, and other similar roles where you are expected to deliver quality services to clients. Any of these jobs can be done by lawyers like yourself without needing to spend a bunch of money on courses to upskill. I have personally done this and I have seen countless clients and friends transition from legal practice to a variety of careers without additional education or training. If you don't believe me, check out Sarah Cottrell's The Former Lawyer podcast, where she interviews lawyers who have moved on to a variety of interesting jobs outside of the law.[36]

Step 6 – Informational interviews

The next step in figuring out your ideal career is to talk to folks who are already working in that field. Seems easy, right? This part scares some lawyers because they believe that asking for help indicates vulnerability and that is not an acceptable state to be in as a lawyer. I'd like to flip that thought around and ask you how many times have others come to you for a help? We're lawyers, after all, this is what we do. If you're still uncomfortable asking someone for 30 minutes of their time, then make a pact with yourself that you will pay it forward the next time someone reaches out to you for an informational interview. If you end up talking to three people, for instance, then promise yourself that you will return this favor to three others. This is good karma, anyway!

The best way to approach informational interviews is to first look for mutual connections. This is super easy to do on LinkedIn, but you can also leverage your real-life lawyer friends and ask them to make an introduction. Again, you will eventually do this for someone else, so don't feel bad about asking for help. Most of your friends will gladly make the connection for you. Once you have identified a few individuals you'd like to talk to, I suggest compiling a list of questions ahead of time. Not only does this give you topics to discuss with your interviewee, but it also shows that you are mindful of their time. Some questions I suggest include:

1. What is one aspect of your job that has surprised you— positive or negative?
2. What are the top three skills you believe are required to succeed in this role?
3. What has been your favorite project so far?

4. What are the most common/typical tasks you perform on a daily basis?

You can of course ask a variety of other questions, but I would stay away from vague topics like "Tell me about your job." If someone wanted to know about what being a lawyer is like, what types of questions would you want that person to ask you in order to get substantive and helpful responses? Think of your informational interview like a friendly deposition, but less transactional. Anyone with whom you speak could eventually turn into a business contact, a referral, or even a future employer.

When I was entertaining the idea of going into law firm administration, I bugged a lot of people who had jobs I was interested in. I mostly did this by reaching out to them on LinkedIn (my favorite, if you can't tell already), but I was also lucky to have a few connections at other firms. I will never forget the wonderfully gracious help I received from the Chief Strategy Officer of a firm where my friend worked. She put me in contact with this woman and we eventually had a few meetings, where she went above and beyond in helping me put together a proposal for my firm to work on the aforementioned new practice area development. The Chief Strategy Officer spent a few hours reviewing my proposal, doing market research on similar roles, and connecting me with another person who had a similar role that I was pursuing. As a small thank you for her assistance, I found out from my friend that she loved to cook, so I sent her a set of artisanal olive oils. I am not suggesting that you do the same for every informational interview you conduct, but if someone goes out of his or her way to help you, then a thoughtful gift might be warranted. At the very least, send a thank you note. People always remember them.

B. Building a Life Around the Vision

Once you have the vision for your career, the next set of steps involves designing your life in such a way that it supports the lifestyle you want. Throughout this book, I keep reinforcing the notion that our personal and work lives are intertwined. Gone are the days where one would leave work at work because there was a clear demarcation between the job that happened during business hours and the family life that occurred before and after. Lawyers especially cannot separate the two given the demands of our careers and our slightly neurotic brains, so it becomes futile to even try. Instead, I urge you to be intentional not just about what job you choose, but also about how you build your life around this career. Who is Adriana, the former lawyer, the coach, the daughter, the wife, the dog mom, the friend, the aunt, the yogi, the athlete, the writer? I am the same person in all facets of my life. Integrating all these parts is more seamless than trying to divorce them and delegate each into its own isolated corner.

Being intentional about how you show up at work and at home requires some planning. Generic goals and aspirations fall by the wayside because, even with the best intentions, we are not very skilled at carrying out the daily tasks necessary to get us to the finish line. I always say that small wins carry the day when it comes to goal setting, but folks have a hard time not seeing huge results right away. It's difficult to stay consistently motivated when it seems like you're just making microscopic improvements. This is why writing down your objectives *and* making a plan for how you will accomplish them are necessary here. I want to start this next section with a dream: if you were totally in charge of your schedule and could design the perfect workweek, what would it look like?

Step 1 – Create your ideal week

The power in creating your ideal week is that it gives you a glimpse of what it's possible. You might not attain it entirely, but you will be able to implement portions of it if you wish. As with the rest of the exercises in this book, the ultimate goal is not perfection, but rather reality made better. The first step in doing so is to list out all of the tasks (both personal and professional) that you generally perform in a week. You don't need to get super granular and include taking a shower or brushing your teeth, but if you take your son to daycare Monday through Friday, that's an item that will inevitably end up in your week. It might not be an ideal errand, but it's your reality and you have to work with it. Alternatively, if one recurring task in your current weekly schedule is taking notes during your team standup meeting even though there are more junior lawyers in attendance and you only do it because you were "voluntold" to do it three years ago, then maybe you give this one up. Maybe it's finally time you delegate this one to someone else. And this is how the ideal week is made.

As an example, I'd like to share with you my ideal week from earlier in the year. I should add that your ideal weeks will change because your priorities and jobs change over time. As with most exercises in this book, they are meant to keep up with your life as it unfolds rather than be used just for a snapshot in time. You will also notice that I am quite generous with listing the hours in each day so that I can give myself some wiggle room. I am not, after all, a drill sergeant. So below is my ideal week from January 2024:

Day / Time	Monday	Tuesday	Wednesday	Thursday	Friday	Saturday	Sunday
6 am	Walk dog, then walk myself Workout Breakfast and get ready for the day	Walk dog, then walk myself Workout Breakfast and get ready for the day	Walk dog, then walk myself Workout Breakfast and get ready for the day	Walk dog, then walk myself Workout Breakfast and get ready for the day	Walk dog, then walk myself Workout Breakfast and get ready for the day	Long walk by myself and stretches Breakfast and get ready for the day	Long workout Big Sunday breakfast

Day / Time	Monday	Tuesday	Wednesday	Thursday	Friday	Saturday	Sunday
9 am	Start workday / Check emails from night before / Plan day	Start workday / Check emails from night before / Plan day	Start workday / Check emails from night before / Plan day	Start workday / Check emails from night before / Plan day	Start workday / Check emails from night before / Plan day	Dog park	Dog park or dog beach
11 am	Deep work / Schedule interviews or seminars for the week	Deep work or work on book	Admin work	Deep work or work on book	Work on book / Prepare for coaching client meetings	Meal prep and grocery shop for the week	Tidy the house
Lunch	Lunch without phone	Lunch without phone	Lunch with husband	Lunch without phone	Lunch without phone	Lunch with husband	Takeout lunch with husband

Day / Time	Monday	Tuesday	Wednesday	Thursday	Friday	Saturday	Sunday
2 pm	Interviews	Interviews or presentation to associates	Meeting with my business coach	Interviews or presentation to associates	Coaching clients	Catch up with family and friends	Chill
4 pm	End of the day ritual / Plan for next day	End of the day ritual / Plan for next day	End of the day ritual / Plan for next day	End of the day ritual / Plan for next day	Coaching clients	Chill	Prepare big Sunday meal
6 pm	Dinner / Catch up with news / Check emails one last time	Dinner / Catch up with news / Check emails one last time	Dinner / Catch up with news / Check emails one last time	Dinner / Catch up with news / Check emails one last time	Out to dinner	Out to dinner	Dinner
Night	In bed by 8 pm; no phone allowed	In bed by 8 pm; no phone allowed	In bed by 8 pm; no phone allowed	In bed by 8 pm; no phone allowed	In bed around 8	In bed after dinner	In bed by 8 pm; no phone allowed

If you are reading my ideal week and thinking that I am the world's most boring person, point taken. Of course there is some variety in my days as sometimes I travel (for fun and for work), sometimes outside forces mess up my perfectly planned week, and every once in a while, life is unpredictable and we need to adjust. I don't follow this schedule 100% of the time, but in a typical week, I do try to abide by the time blocks I created. It truly helps me envision my week ahead with much more clarity than if I was just diving in on a Monday to whatever was lobbed my way. It also keeps me on track for my big projects, such as writing this book. It's a common misconception that writers simply put words to paper daily and then, voila! a book is born. Writing takes a lot of planning, outlining, researching, thinking, drafting, and erasing ideas. Although the ideal week above simply states "work on book," there is a lot more to the process than just writing.

Which brings me to my next point: batching. Man, do I love batching my days! Ever heard of batching? In its simplest form, batching means grouping similar activities together in a certain scheduled timeframe. The opposite of batching is doing whatever work grabs your attention first, switching from task to task until your brain is all jumbled and you feel like you haven't been able to focus on a single project all day. I honestly can't imagine trying to write a book (or a motion or client engagement letter or a contract) if I was constantly toggling between it and my emails and my phone and another intense writing assignment. And yet, many of you probably operate this way! My friends, you don't have to. The easiest way to avoid this trap is by scheduling when you want to work on similar tasks. For instance, you might set aside an hour or two every morning to read and respond to emails, then an hour to work on something that requires focus, and then a couple of hours in the afternoon for meetings. This way, you're not going from reading one email to trying to finish a motion to then jumping on a client call, then reading the emails that came through while you were on the call, while simultaneously researching case law for your motion. Our attention spans—short as they may be—really do not like being pulled in multiple directions at once. You will always be more productive by concentrating on a single task at a time. Plus, it is much easier to capture your billable work when you batch! It's truly a double win.

As you can imagine, there are multiple ways to batch your days but the best way will always be the way you are most likely to follow. It's tempting to look at my ideal schedule or someone else's example and want to immediately adopt it for yourself, but if it doesn't support your work reality, then you won't stick with it for long. So start by tracking how you currently spend your days. What do your mornings look like? What about afternoons and evenings? Do you see any patterns in terms of when you have the most energy, when you feel drained, when the majority of meetings happen, or when deadlines fall? Regardless of the job, we all have these recurring items in our schedules, and as long as you can identify them, you can start pairing them with similar tasks so that you can work on specific aspects of your job at scheduled times. If you feel the most focused in the mornings, then perhaps you could block your calendar then so you can do high-impact work, and postpone meetings to the afternoon. On the other hand, if you take a while to get going in the morning, that may be your ideal time for administrative work or emails.

Some folks who have more control of their schedules (like law firm owners, independent contractors, or even lawyers who are highly specialized in an area) can experiment with batching their entire week:

- On Monday, you might work on client prospecting and business development in addition to reading and responding to emails.

- On Tuesday, you might do deep work plus emails.

- On Wednesday, you might have all of your meetings plus emails.

- On Thursday, you work on projects that require deep work or respond to client requests.

- On Friday, you plan for the next week and do the administrative work required to move your client work forward.

This is where the next step comes in. Every single goal—no matter how big or small—must be broken down into smaller chunks in order to be doable. If you say to yourself "This year, I will write a book" and you make no daily plan to get this book done, it's not happening. I know because I was there. I've wanted to write a book for as long as I can remember, but it wasn't until I decided to carve out time to put my idea to paper and block that time in my calendar, that it morphed from a concept to an achievable project. I implemented the same process for writing this book, as I have for other goals I've set out for myself. It's not rocket science, but so many of us become so intimidated by our own goals that we abandon them before we make even the smallest progress. It's easier to say that you got busy than to admit that you got scared.

Step 2 – Break down goals into daily and weekly to-do lists

So how do we take goals and break them down into daily and weekly tasks? I like to think of goals as having three phases: preparation, substantive work, and wrap-up. In the preparation phase, you gather data, set a completion date, and create a plan for tackling your goal. Warning: this is when most goals die. As lawyers, we are enamored with researching and future-proofing our ideas, but then we get overwhelmed by the options and our perfectionism kicks in, so we give up before we even get started. James Clear talks about 1% improvement: if you get better at something by just 1% each day, that compounds on the progress you made yesterday and in the span of a year, your results will be nearly 37 times better than when you first started.[37] This is a frustrating concept for most of us because these 1% improvements don't seem to make much of a difference in the short term. But the inverse is also true: making poor choices at a 1% margin compounds in the future to eventually become huge missteps. As Clear puts it, "Making a choice that is 1 percent better or 1 percent worse seems insignificant in the moment, but over the span of moments that make up a lifetime these choices determine the difference between who you are and who you could be."[38]

Now that we have prepared for our goal, we move on to the substantive step. This is where we break down our monumental ambition into bitesize daily and weekly tasks. Let's say you decide to open your own law firm within a year. I have never owned a law firm myself, but even with this deficit, I can tell you that you will likely need the following: an area of practice, client leads (note I did not say actual clients because that isn't necessary before starting a law firm), and the administrative components of running a law firm (a trust account, a name, a website, a computer, perhaps an office, etc.). While this may sound like an imposing to-do list, how do you eat an elephant? One bite at a time!

Below follows how I might break down the goal of opening my own law firm into weekly and daily tasks, while also working a full-time job. Every week, your goal should be to accomplish one task related to opening your law firm. Some weeks, this might be a huge feat like completing your new website, while other weeks, it might look like writing half of a business plan. You can't measure your progress by the difficulty of the task, but rather by the consistency of your work toward the goal. I know this is where you're going to start laughing uncontrollably because you don't believe this can possibly be done, but this is how the vast majority of lawyers start their own law firms: they work for someone else, then they decide they could do it better on their own, and they plan and take small steps until they are ready to hang their shingle. No one takes a year-long vacation to prepare to open a law firm. Most don't have the financial backing or the experience to get a firm up and running in a week.

So let's eat the elephant one bite at a time:

Weekly plan	Daily plan
Week 1 – Decide on a practice area for your law firm	Monday – list out matters you have worked on throughout your career that you have enjoyed the most Tuesday – list your biggest accomplishments in your cases to date Wednesday – spend an hour or less researching other solo attorneys in your geographical area who specialize in a similar practice Thursday – from the list of lawyers you compiled on Wednesday, compile a couple of names who might become referrals down the road and a few attorneys who are 10 years ahead of where you'd like to be to provide an idea of what types of cases they have handled in order to keep their law firm running Friday – create a new bio as if you already run your own law firm, identifying your past successes and practice concentration. Note: this doesn't need to be perfect or reflect the final iteration of your firm website.

| Week 2 – Build out an expertise | Monday – from the list of lawyers who practice in a similar area that you hope to practice, identify how they market their expertise, such as writing articles, maintaining a blog, hosting webinars, or engaging in local community events

Tuesday – choose a couple of methods from the above to begin building out your expertise. I would advise against trying to do all the things and instead pick just one or two methods that you know you would enjoy and be able to stick with long-term.

Wednesday – out of the methods you have chosen, practice one today—that might look like writing an article or a blog or recording a short video

Thursday – repeat Wednesday's exercise

Friday – create a schedule of content that feels doable. Warning: don't get overly ambitious or you will burn out quickly. Remember that small pieces of content posted on a regular schedule win out over extensive knowledge pieces that you only release once or twice a year. |

Week 3 – Begin working on client leads	Monday – identify current or former clients who would be a good fit for your future law firm
	Tuesday – write personalized emails to each client informing them that you are starting your new practice, reminding them of the work you performed for them in the past and inviting them to call you should they need help in the future. Note: you are not contacting them at this moment; you are simply preparing an index of future potential clients at this point.
	Wednesday – identify other lawyers or professionals (such as accountants, family mediators, counselors, physicians, business owners, etc.) who might serve as future referral partners
	Thursday – write personalized emails to each potential referral source informing them of your new law firm. Note: you are not sending these out right now.
	Friday – identify other contacts (besides lawyers or potential referral partners) who are natural connectors and love making introductions in order to expand your network once you are getting ready to open your law firm

If the above examples give you heartburn, please understand that they are just for illustrative purposes. There is no official manual on starting a law firm, just as none exists for setting and achieving other goals. You don't have to follow this advice on a daily basis— you can certainly space it out and improvise as time allows. The larger point here is that any long-term goals can be (and should be) broken down into daily bitesize tasks that you can commit to and maintain until you achieve your goal. Each item I mentioned above can be accomplished in an hour or less, but you can also break everything down even further into 30-minute increments if that feels more doable. You can also extrapolate the process of starting a firm to any other ambitious endeavor, like making partner at your current firm or transitioning out of the law or running a marathon or becoming a social media influencer. The process is the same.

What if you're not working toward a major goal right now? That's okay, you might be in the season of smaller-scale pursuits. Speaking of seasons, productivity expert Cal Newport writes in his most recent book *Slow Productivity: The Lost Art of Accomplishment Without Burnout* that working seasonally is one of the keys to avoiding burnout. He explains that part of the problem with today's knowledge workers (including lawyers and other office-type professionals) is that we are always working "at a constant state of anxious high energy, with little change, throughout the whole entire year."[39] He recommends scheduling rest periods to match with the seasons, if possible, or just throughout the week. If you think about the school year for example, it operates seasonally: we start classes in the fall, take a winter vacation, begin a new semester in the spring, and go on summer vacation. Of course, most of our jobs don't operate like this (I mean, could you imagine going to summer camp as an adult? It's both thrilling and terrifying.), but there is room to implement this concept. Most of us begin our legal jobs after we take the bar exam in the summer, so the fall is a natural starting season for lawyers. Personally, I look at the fall as a time to wake up from the usually slower summer season. I like to publish books and articles in the fall, as well as launch my group coaching program to begin in the fall. It's a time for learning and upskilling, much like we did in school. And if you have children, why not adopt a "back to school" mentality alongside them?

In the winter, we Floridians turn into those lizards who just freeze on the side of the road until the sun can warm us up again. Just kidding; however, I do like to take winters slow and focus on family time, especially around the holidays. When the new year kicks in, I don't follow the trend of setting a resolution. Instead, I wait until my birthday in February to create an intention for my next age. For instance, when I turned 35, I decided I wanted to leave the law. When I turned 36, I wanted to write a book. The following year, I would start a business. Working toward that goal usually begins in the spring, which is a great time for renewal. Similar to the fall, I feel energized and ready to tackle big projects in the spring. Summers for me signal a time for reflection as we approach the halfway mark in the year. I like to look back on the first part of the year and ask myself "How do I want to move forward in the second half?" The summer is also secretly the best time to look for jobs, as many candidates are on vacation, so competition is slimmer than usual. If you plan on changing positions before year-end, the summer is a great time to begin.

As you can probably tell, there are many variations to using the seasons to make quarterly plans, especially if you're not working toward a larger overarching goal. There is a natural beginning and end to each season, providing a perfect window for reaching smaller-scale objectives. How might you apply the concept of seasonality to your life?

Step 3 – Boundaries

The concept of boundaries has been discussed ad nauseam in the legal profession. It's often described as a means for newer attorneys to refuse work in the name of #balance, leaving the senior lawyers to do everything themselves while they angrily wave their fists at these lazy young'uns. But this is too simplistic and doesn't accurately reflect the realities of practicing law. The dictionary definition of boundary is "something that indicates or fixes a limit or extent."[40] The truth is that every single human has a limit or extent, even if it's measured subjectively. None of us can or should be expected to work beyond our limits. Pushing back on what we perceive as an encroachment to our limit is an act of self-preservation and self-respect. The fact that one person's limit appears more expansive than another person's does not make it the absolute truth. And our limits aren't stagnant; they shift and vary as we move through life and experience the many peaks and valleys thrown our way. So why is the concept of boundaries subject to such a narrow discussion, limited to the dichotomy of those who have boundaries and should be demonized versus those who apparently don't have any boundaries (a factual impossibility) and should be praised?

A chill lawyer has boundaries *and* knows when and how to exert them. A chill lawyer also knows that today's boundary may not be tomorrow's or next week's boundary. A chill lawyer holds values firmly but has a flexible outlook depending on the circumstances. Knowing what matters most and what actions are necessary to achieve that are paramount to creating boundaries that others observe. They may not agree with them and they might feel inconvenienced by them, but when you can articulate your end goal in conjunction with setting a boundary, people are much more likely to respect you and honor your limits. When I was starting out as a lawyer, I developed a reputation for saying yes to every assignment. I didn't know how to say no because I honestly had nothing else to focus on. Work was everything to me back then, partly because I grew up poor and was desperate to stay out of poverty and partly because I hadn't really developed any hobbies or friendships with my co-workers. So all I did was work.

Eventually, I burned out, of course I did. But more importantly, I created a system of values and priorities in my life that gave me direction and something else to work toward besides my job.

I started exercising consistently, traveling with my husband, and reconnecting with my college and law school friends. I also started to develop skills that were law-adjacent, even if not necessarily required for my job. All of these activities not only enhanced my personal and professional life and offered me a trajectory as a young adult, but they also became my shield against boundary-pushers. No longer did I feel the need to say yes solely due to a lack of alternatives; now I had lots of other things I could do *and* I learned how to verbalize my boundaries in a way that didn't make me seem lazy or unmotivated. When I felt that I had reached my limit and someone assigned me another project, I would say something along the lines of:

> Thank you for thinking of me for X project. You know I've enjoyed working with you in the past and I'm looking forward to working together again; however, I have to decline this assignment with the stated deadline. I am currently working on Y and Z projects for Lawyer 1 and Lawyer 2, and I'd hate to not be able to do my best work for all three of you. In addition, I have already committed to this personal activity/trip and unfortunately, I cannot reschedule.

Then I would throw in a lifesaver line at the end of the email to indicate that I would be happy to work on this project after a certain date if it was still available. You would be surprised how many deadlines aren't actually deadlines and if the assignment really is interesting, you might as well push out the date of your availability and see if the other person bites. I have also seen partners call the other partners mentioned in the email and ask that they release me from their projects so I could work on theirs. It's not the savviest move, but I always remained an innocent party in the argument. The response I laid out above accomplishes several things: it shows gratitude for the assignment, genuine admiration for the sender and desire to work together again, and a thorough explanation of other priorities. Unless the partner is a total bully (in which case, run!), he or she will appreciate the information and will respect your boundary.

Boundaries aren't always against external forces; sometimes, you need to limit your own habits. A former co-worker was such a people-pleaser to the point that she often ended up overcommitted, juggling multiple committees and volunteering events that frankly interfered with her actual work. She had several meetings with partners who told her point-blank that she would need to choose between her job and all these extracurriculars. I asked her why she did so much outside of work—thinking that she just hated being a lawyer and was desperately trying to escape—and she just broke down crying. It turns out she never intended to be so overly involved with all of these non-profits, but they kept asking more and more of her and she just couldn't turn it down. Through tears, she sobbed that it made her feel loved and appreciated. She was terrified to let anyone down, so she just piled on more and more commitments. My co-worker needed to learn that she was her own boundary-pusher. None of these organizations forced her into extensive involvement; she guilted herself into doing so much.

Without judgment or shame, can you find an instance in which you violated your own boundary? Was there a core value that you didn't respect? A priority that you let slip away? If another person had tried to do this to you, how would you have responded? In my co-worker's case, she had to reestablish her limits and practice respecting her own time before agreeing to take on any additional obligations. She had to allow herself to feel a little guilty when saying no in order to fully participate in the next endeavor she would say yes to.

Step 4 – Detach from distractions

When I think of ways in which I break my boundaries, social media is at the top. During the pandemic, I went into a deep social media hole. Bored and anxious about the world, I would spend hours scrolling through my phone. I checked my phone's settings one day and to my absolute horror, I had spent over six hours on my phone. Six! I have mostly dug myself out of that habit, but it wasn't easy and I couldn't rely on willpower alone. Willpower only takes you so far and it's usually not that far. You are literally having to will yourself every single time to *not* do something. It's very challenging. Then if you fail just one time, your brain says "Okay, you broke the streak. Let's stop doing it."

Instead, I had to rely on automation to help me in removing these distractions so that they wouldn't take up any mental space and I wouldn't have to make a daily decision to *not* do something. If you also struggle with over-indulging in social media, here is what I did that may help you break loose:

Step 1 – Phone

I first tackled my iPhone because it is both our best tool and our biggest productivity crutch. I don't have to remind you of all the studies showing that our phones impact our sleep, our cognitive abilities, our creativity, attention span, and time with our families. These little buggers get between us and living our lives. I often wish I could just go back to an old-school "dumb" phone so that I wouldn't feel the need to use mine so frequently, but then I remembered the usefulness of smart devices and instead decided that limiting my usage would be the next best thing.

So in my phone's settings, I limit my screen time before 7:00 am and after 7:00 pm, meaning that I can't access any of my phone's features during the off times. I cannot read my email, open any applications, read the news, or play games. Before 7:00 am and after 7:00 pm, my phone's only function is to make calls. What this setting has accomplished is remove my ability to decide on my own whether or not I read emails as soon as I wake up or check Instagram before bed. I now wake up and go to bed without my phone stealing my attention. It is quite Zen.

I told this story to a lawyer friend and he almost fell out of his chair. He actually couldn't believe how simple it was to stop himself from compulsively looking at his phone first thing in the morning or right before bed. He called me about a week after he implemented this setting, downright giddy about the fact that he no longer reached for his phone until 7:00 am in the morning because he had gotten used to the fact that his phone offered no entertainment before that time. And that's the best part: eventually, your brain just adapts to this new setting and you won't even look for your phone outside of the hours you set. It's pure magic!

The biggest obstacle lawyers have with this feature is the fear that they can't be reached during a work emergency. To soothe your anxiety, you have two options: (1) you can make an exception and check your work email in the evening before bed (just make sure you *only* check your email and you do so for a predetermined amount of time, like 30 minutes), and (2) you can remind yourself that your phone still works and if something is truly an emergency, you will receive a call. I mean, seriously, no one will send you 20 frantic emails in a row without calling you at some point if you don't answer. Sometimes our brains play anxious little games with us that aren't based in reality.

Step 2 – Social Media

The second addiction I had to tackle was my social media usage. Again, I knew I couldn't just stop myself from spending hours on Facebook, Instagram or Reddit, and I had seen too many friends delete the apps altogether only to reinstall them months later and start the cycle again. So I relied on my phone's settings to restrict my ability to use these apps to only 10 minutes a day *combined*. That's right, your phone can put a time limit on any application and once you reach that limit, it will automatically shut it off. I know 10 minutes seems extreme, so you can start with an hour and slowly reduce the time. But the point is to give yourself a hard boundary on the apps that you waste the most time on without having to rely on self-control every day.

Honestly, some days I bypass the restriction and use Instagram for longer, but most of the time, I stay within the allotted 10 minutes. As you might imagine, I have become extremely efficient at checking the big announcements and making sure I don't miss birthdays, then when my time is up, I just move on with my day. Rarely do I wish I had more time because, let's face it, the information we see on social media isn't really groundbreaking. The algorithm demons have dumbed down our feeds so they're not as exciting nowadays. Eventually your fear of missing out what's happening in the socials dissipates and you realize that, in fact, nothing is really happening.

Step 3 – Email

Emails are tricky because this is what we do as lawyers: email back and forth. It may seem like a productive use of our time because it's such a widely accepted method of communication in the workplace but think about the last time an email actually resolved a problem. More often than not, we create more issues by sending poorly worded emails and responding with a vague one-sentence answer, which then causes the sender to ask for clarification, which then annoys us, and we have to respond with even more nonsense. And we do this until it's 6:00 pm and the workday is finished, but we haven't really accomplished that much. Sound familiar? When people say that this meeting should've been an email, I think that most emails should be a 30-second phone call that actually settles the matter.

Reducing the amount of time spent on emails seems like a Herculean feat—and it mostly is—but I have a few tips if you'd like to give it a try:

1. Check email a few times a day. My biggest tip for not getting sucked into emails all day is to set certain times during the

day when you open your email and respond. For instance, you could do this at 7:00 am, 9:00 am, 11:00 am, after lunch, 2:00 pm, 4:00 pm, and at some point before bed. I know this suggestion makes some of you break out in hives, but I promise that your emails aren't going anywhere just because you don't read them the second they come in. No one actually expects you to respond within a minute of receiving an email. And think about it: if you are reading emails as soon as they come in, you're essentially allowing other people to dictate how you spend your time. And why would you do that?

2. Put emails into three buckets: respond, deal with later, or delete. When you do choose to read your emails, think about which ones actually need a response right now versus ones that can wait. Sometimes in our frantic days when we are bombarded by emails, we feel like we must respond to every single one, which not only wastes time, but also leads to sending half-assed emails in a hurry that only cause more confusion and back-and-forth. When we do this, we operate in reactive mode. Oftentimes the better course of action is to flag certain emails and give yourself time to respond more thoughtfully. You could even schedule this time in your calendar, perhaps toward the end of the day before you wrap up your work. Emails that are junk or just FYI should be deleted right away. If it later turns out that you needed that information, you can always search for it in your deleted emails. Otherwise, a clean inbox is so much prettier.

3. Use rules. I'm always shocked by the number of lawyers who don't make use of the rules feature in Microsoft Outlook, which allows you to create subfolders for particular cases, clients, partners, or personal emails and then associate a keyword with each subfolder so that all emails containing that keyword go to their designated folder. If you handle cases, this is the easiest way to stay organized. Simply create

a subfolder with each case name and generate a rule that includes that case name in the subject of any email, so that all your correspondence on that particular case will be in a subfolder in your inbox. You never have to search thousands of emails for case information once you implement this. And once again, you end up with a pretty inbox!

C. Executing on Your Vision

When I was in my seventh year of practice, I got an itch I couldn't scratch. I felt like I was on a conveyor belt of litigating in a specific practice area and I couldn't get off. I didn't know what was on the other side of that conveyor belt, but I really didn't like what was ahead of me. I started to look for jobs, with no particular set of requirements in mind. (Warning: if you catch yourself doing this, stop. Your time is much better spent creating your list of likes/dislikes/tolerates, strengths, values, and other self-learning tools versus blindly searching the internet for a job that magically solves all of your problems.). Of course a job popped up—one that I had no business taking. It was at another firm, doing a slightly different type of litigation. The managing partner recruited me hard, promising me interesting work, independence, and a generous bonus program. I remember trying to hype myself up on the way to interview, feigning excitement for all the cases I would be expected to handle. I actually didn't want any of this, but I didn't allow myself to think beyond working as a lawyer. My brain was in full denial mode that the itch wouldn't be scratched by another job at a different, but ultimately very similar, law firm.

A few weeks into this job, I knew it wasn't right. I dreaded going to the office and pretending like I cared about my clients and my cases. I did mediocre work. I forgot deadlines, I botched motions, I half-assed mediations. A generally prolific writer, I wrote my worst article on a topic I could care less about. If I wasn't able to find this article online today, I honestly couldn't even tell you what it was about. My colleagues were fine, but I was unable to muster any interest in the firm as a whole. We had a firm retreat during my short tenure there and I can't remember the names of any of the lawyers I met during it. I lasted there six months and quit without another job lined up. It's easily the lowest and most embarrassing experience of my entire career. I wish I could wipe it off my resume and out of memory. More than that, I wish I could go back and tell myself that this itch couldn't be scratched by just changing jobs.

Why am I telling you this story all the way at the end of the book? Because I am not perfect. Despite my chill lawyer mantra, I too revert to the frantic job-hunting that promises to solve all my problems. It's sometimes easier than doing the inner work to figure out *why* I'm unhappy or anxious or unfulfilled. But, as you can see from my experience, it can quickly devolve into a crappy work experience that damages you even more than if you had stayed put and taken the time to ask yourself what you need. If you do decide that a new job is warranted, let it come from a need for growth and for exciting opportunities rather than despair.

And the first step is to articulate exactly what you are looking for. A new job should provide (1) the right circumstances for expanding or acquiring new skills, (2) a more beneficial financial structure, and/or (3) an improved leadership. You do not need all three in order to make a move; however, it's helpful if the new job allows you to make progress in all three categories. Note that I was careful in how I worded the financial aspect as I don't believe that all new jobs need to come with a higher paycheck. I have taken pay cuts when the number of hours I worked also went down, thus resulting in a significantly higher hourly wage and more free time; conversely, the job that paid me the most on its face was also the most stressful job I ever had and ultimately not worth the money. These aren't universal truths, of course, but they do merit a discussion since more money isn't always better. What you should look for instead is something that aligns with your personality and skills, the ability to work with people you like and value, and a compensation package that makes sense given your expected duties.

The best time to look for a job is when you don't need one and the best way to find a job is by asking your friends. It's mind-boggling how many lawyers at this very moment are searching for a new position, meanwhile their friends are also doing the same and they just don't talk about it. What if your buddy interviewed for a role that wasn't right for him, but might be ideal for you? Wouldn't your friend recommend you for it? This exact scenario happened to me—once I referred a former co-worker to a job I didn't accept and as far as I know, she still happily works there now, and another time, I was the recipient of a job opportunity after my friend's firm offered her a bunch of money to prevent her from quitting. It can be a win all around, but only if you share with your friends that you're job searching. One caveat: be delicate when it comes to current co-workers even if they seem really cool; snitches are everywhere.

Going back to LinkedIn and the many reasons to build an online network, one direct benefit is the ability to reach out to a contact if you see that his or her employer posted a job you're interested in and ask for an introduction. Not only do many companies offer referral bonuses to employees, but it builds goodwill for your connection to help bring on a new hire. It might be uncomfortable to ask, but if you have completed the self-assessment I suggested earlier in this book and you realize that you'd be a great fit for this role, you're not even asking for a favor—you're actually doing the company a favor by presenting yourself as a candidate. Trust me, as someone who has hired dozens of lawyers in my career, I wish the perfect candidate would just appear so that I can stop reviewing blah resumes and interviewing subpar applicants. And even if you don't end up getting this job, your LinkedIn contact might refer you for an even better position in the future. People love helping other people (despite what horrible stories we hear about lawyers sometimes).

Because I love making lists and helping you stay organized, here is how I would designate my own job search:

- Create some parameters of your must-haves in a job so that you stay on track and don't get distracted by seemingly sexy jobs that don't meet your requirements.

- Tell your closest lawyer friends and other trusted referral sources what you're looking for (be as specific as possible so when they hear about the perfect job, they automatically think of you).

- Clean up your online presence and social media, especially if you've been at the same job for several years and haven't applied for a new position recently.

- Schedule an hour per week to look through job postings, limiting your search to those posted in the prior week as many companies repost their jobs periodically even if they have already filled them. It annoys me to no end, but it's the truth.

- Tailor your resume and cover letter specifically to the job you are applying for, even if it takes an extra 20 minutes to do so. The difference between a resume that grabs the hiring manager's attention and one that gets tossed is often in whether the job posting is mirrored in the resume by using key words.

There are lots of books out there on interviewing tips, so I will not pile on top of that advice, but I want to add a few tips from the interviewer side. The first is quite simple: create a short and strong answer to the question "Why do you want to work here?" because you will be inevitably asked this within the first few minutes of the interview. This question shouldn't catch you by surprise and while you don't want to sound rehearsed, you want to come off as confident and prepared. When crafting your response, focus on what is pulling you toward this specific job as opposed to what is pushing you away from your current job. Prospective employers don't care that you hate your job or manager or that the hours are terrible; they want to know what you will bring to the table.

Most legal interviews are designed to assess your problem-solving skills so you will inevitably get questions about how you have tackled challenges in the past and how you've managed difficult clients or co-workers. You have to tread carefully here, as firm-bashing or even worse, client-shaming, is not tolerated in the legal industry. You can give a concrete example without naming names or even offering a timeframe, which would allow the interviewer to match it to the employer during that time. At the end of the day, the interviewer isn't looking for juicy gossip; he or she is simply trying to evaluate your ability to find solutions, act pragmatically in a charged situation, and deliver results for your clients. Don't overthink this prompt and don't over-explain.

If you are like me, you may have quite a few jobs listed in your resume. While changing jobs has become much more acceptable since the pandemic, you will likely still get asked to explain why you left each position. Again, you shouldn't be caught off-guard or attacked by these questions; instead, create a timeline of your jobs that flows and highlights your professional development. If you started out as a general litigation associate and then moved on to a more niche practice area, you can explain what skills you were missing that you were able to gain in the new role. If you worked at a firm, then moved in-house and now you're applying for a firm again, you can rationalize the boomerang by pointing out specific aspects of firm work that you enjoyed and would like to return to. The bottom line is that every move should have a story attached to it so that the interviewer can understand your motivations.

My final piece of advice on interviewing is to avoid dancing around the compensation question. There is a lot of guidance out there on whether you should offer a number first or how to package your experience to increase the dollar value, but at the of the day, firms and other employers that do not operate on a lockstep plan have a ton of leeway in structuring salaries and bonuses. If they like you and see a future for you, they will pay you. Everything is negotiable, but you have to be in the same ballpark. An employer that quibbles with you over $10,000 or $20,000 is probably going to make you wish you hadn't accepted the job. You don't need to have a magic number in mind to make a move, but do express your compensation requirements clearly and unequivocally during the interview. I know many of us grew up learning that discussing money is taboo, but now we're adults with bills and student loans, so let's go after it.

One of the first actions a recruiter or interviewer will take once you submit your application is to look you up on LinkedIn. Most lawyers have a LinkedIn profile, but it contains the bare minimum of information: current and prior jobs, schools attended, the firm headshot, and current city. There is so much more to add, not just for potential employers, but also for clients and other business relationships. You can spend a lot of time customizing your page, but here are the most visible portions:

1. Your headline—this is essentially your professional tagline to signal to the world what you do and what you're about. Some folks have really gone overboard with the descriptors to add emojis and generic phrases like "changemaker" and "purpose-driven." Too many words dilute your headline, so stick to the basics: what type of law you practice and something to grab the attention of your ideal clients, like a concentration, a niche, an important achievement that sets you apart from others, or a unique aspect of your background.

2. Your featured section—this is pinned to your profile and will always appear when someone views it. If you have written an article or been highlighted in a news story or posted

something that got a lot of traction, these posts would be perfect for this section.

3. Your "About" section—this is the longest of the three and it's akin to your bio. It shouldn't necessarily read like a resume, but I am a big fan of breaking it down into sections, such as accomplishments, top skills, and personal details, so that the viewer doesn't have to muddle through long paragraphs.

Also, remember to keep your contact information up to date, as well as refresh your headshot every few years. For lawyers, I also recommend including publications and certifications, but they certainly aren't required.

Finally, I want to talk about vocation. Some of you may find something you're so passionate about that it literally blends your soul with your work. Working toward something you love—a passion— can be motivating on a level you've never experienced before. There is a saying about entrepreneurs: they avoid working 40 hours for a boss so they can work 80 hours a week for themselves. The grind somehow feels different when you are calling the shots and building your own dream. It's both harder and more rewarding. I never considered starting a business until I left the practice of law. Suddenly I had more energy and more time to think about how I could relay the lessons I learned in the past decade to help other lawyers. It started with writing a book, which then morphed into a coaching business, all while still working a full-time job as director of professional development. While I haven't been as intentional about growing The Chill Lawyer as other coaches, I nonetheless feel a love for it akin to birthing a child. I want it to thrive, to help others, and to leave a legacy when I'm gone. I have learned more from building this business than I ever did in law school and I get more personal satisfaction from working just one hour in my business than I did an entire day as a lawyer. Is it my vocation? Quite possibly.

In his book *Meaningful Work: A Quest to Do Great Business,*

Find Your Calling, and Feed Your Soul, Shawn Askinosie beautifully describes the process of going from a nationally renowned, highly successful criminal defense attorney to a small-batch chocolate maker: after a particularly challenging murder case, he went to give his client some unexpected good news and he broke down crying while his client comforted him.[41] He realized then and there that he no longer wanted to practice law. But he didn't initially listen to this inner voice; instead, he tried other areas of the law and forced himself to continue on the same path he had been on for decades. Until he decided to take inventory of his talents:

> I was really good at cross-examining witnesses in criminal trials; I was even better at cross-examining expert witnesses; and my ultimate skill was cross-examining a law enforcement officer. Awesome. Those skills are totally universally transferable to a plethora of next career choices (not) . . . I didn't have a degree in business, had taken zero accounting classes, had no experience manufacturing, was not mechanical, and wasn't really that great with numbers. Sounds like the recipe for a fantastic leader of a manufacturing business, right? I did have a few transferrable talents, though, like crafting and telling stories (marketing), locating difficult-to-find people (excellent cocoa farmers), and solving complex problems (manufacturing and international business).[42]

Once he stepped away from his practice, Askinosie then allowed himself to process the painful grief over his father's death that he had been suppressing for years. He volunteered, rebuilt his relationship with God, and started cooking and baking. One day—after he stopped obsessing over his next career move—he was driving by his grandparents' old farm and the thought of making chocolate from scratch just popped into his head.[43] The idea seemed out of nowhere, but in reality, it was tied to his upbringing on a farm, his desire to bring joy to kids who had experienced a loss as he did, and to help underserved communities around the world (which he now does through profit-sharing with cocoa farmers, feeding thousands of schoolchildren in Tanzania and the Philippines, and providing work opportunities for at-risk youth in his chocolate factory in Springfield, Missouri). All told, it took him five years to find his passion.

I include this before-and-after story at the very end of my book not only because it is aspirational, but because in his book, Askinosie lays out the exact methods he undertook to find his vocation, many of which are nearly identical to the advice I included in my book. These steps—create a list of your strengths, get clarity by looking inward, follow your interests without expecting immediate returns, stick to a routine, and don't get caught up in what other people are doing—are universal. I didn't invent them and neither did Askinosie. The reason they work is because they are wholly within your power to implement; they are not dependent on any outside factors or some other advantage. You get to decide what to do first, what to do next, and what to skip altogether.

Even if you take every instruction in this book and dutifully complete all the exercises, you may not find your vocation. And you may end up perfectly happy with a perfectly great job anyway. As I've written several times, the journey is more important than the end result. Learning to be introspective, to vocalize what you like and don't like, and to self-assess your strengths and not-so-strengths are not wasted skills. While they may not provide you with an immediate solution or uncover your absolute passion in life, you will have gained a level of awareness and richness about who you are at your very core. You may realize that you actually love being a lawyer or that a job you overlooked in the past was the best fit for you or that entrepreneurship is actually not the dream you envisioned. The journey of life and career is long and full of unexpected twists; knowing thyself will save you from being led astray.

Final Word

In the opening sentence of *Anna Karenina*, Leo Tolstoy famously writes: "All happy families are alike; each unhappy family is unhappy in its own way."[44] While its meaning has been heavily debated by scholars much smarter than me, the gist is that there are certain attributes that form a happy family, while unhappy families are plagued by a number of different factors. The phrase also implies that unhappy families make up a more interesting subject and thus piques the reader's curiosity about the book; after all, who wants to read about a boring, happy family?

Whether or not factually accurate, the same could be said about lawyers: all happy lawyers share a common thread, though not necessarily common characteristics. Happy lawyers know that it is up to them to make their own paths in this career. They learn—through trials and tribulations—that the law works for them, not the other way around. They seek inner guidance before outside opinions. They don't try to fit into a mold that wasn't made for them. Happy lawyers know that chasing glitz and glamour will eventually leave you broken and spiritless. Their health and well-being are paramount. They consistently enrich their lives through inner contemplation, hobbies, movement, activities that feed their soul, and friendships. They never stop learning and growing. They never stop questioning the old guard and the status quo.

If you are an unhappy lawyer or an anxious lawyer or an unfulfilled lawyer, you may be unique in what causes your misery, but you're not alone. Thousands of lawyers struggle in silence, afraid of judgment and of consequences for speaking up. I hope that, at the very least, this book proves that all happy lawyers faced adversity and insecurity at some point. Flowers grow through dirt, diamonds are created under pressure, and butterflies emerge from grimy little caterpillars. All success stories have lows and highs because our lives aren't linear. It's hard to envision a legacy when you're in the muddy part of life, but the present turns into the past in the blink of an eye. Today's difficulties will soon become yesterday's triumphs. Keeping perspective of the long career ahead is a supreme skill for lawyers.

And always remember the chill lawyer maxim:

Confidence

Health

Intuition

Learning, and

Light

I'll be cheering you on, always.
Adriana Paris

Endnotes

1   Adriana M. Paris, *Rising Lawyer: From Summer Associate to First-Year Associate* (West Academic Publishing, 2023).
2   American Bar Association, "Growth of the legal profession," ABA Profile of the Legal Profession 2023, https://www.abalegalprofile.com/demographics.html.
3   National Task Force on Lawyer Well-Being, "The Path to Lawyer Well-Being: Practical Recommendations for Positive Change," August 14, 2017, 7, https://www.americanbar.org/content/dam/aba/administrative/professional_responsibility/lawyer_well_being_report_final.pdf
4   Chelsea Fredlund, "Mental Health by the Numbers: An Infographic Mapping the Legal Industry's Well-Being," May 18, 2023, https://www.law.com/americanlawyer/2023/05/18/mental-health-by-the-numbers-an-infographic-mapping-the-legal-industrys-wellbeing/
5   Greg McKeown, "To Build a Top Performing Team, Ask for 85% Effort," Harvard Business Review, June 8, 2023, https://hbr.org/2023/06/to-build-a-top-performing-team-ask-for-85-effort.
6   *The Bhagavad Gita* (E. Easwaran, Trans.; 2nd ed. 2007), Ch. 2, Verse 47.
7   Yes, writing this book was hard work and included many, many drafts.
8   I am happy to say I never did learn his management style.
9   I will come back to this later but get yourself some non-lawyer friends! They are worth their weight in gold.
10 Tara Mohr, *Playing Big: Practical Wisdom for Women Who Want to Speak Up, Create, and Lead* (New York: Avery, 2015), 43.
11 Yes, I had developed a reputation for writing client-acceptable time entries so other lawyers (including seasoned partners) would ask me to "fix" theirs before submission. I actually enjoyed doing this work—a preview that I would eventually end up in professional development—but I would get overwhelmed because they all wanted their time reviewed at the end of each month.

12 I know some of you are eye-rolling me hard right now, but in my defense, I was in my mid-20s and 50 seemed ancient back then.

13 Fast Company, "Jonathan Fields Drawn to Fast Company's Executive Board's insightful and Highly Curated Community," https://board. fastcompany.com/success-stories/insightful-highly-curated-community-draws-jonathan-fields.

14 Jonathan Fields, The Good Life Project Podcast, "Kelly Corrigan Interviews Me," December 2023, https://www.goodlifeproject.com/podcast/kelly-corrigan-turning-the-tables-on-interviewers-what-happens-when-podcast-hosts-interview-each-other/.

15 Andrew Huberman, The Huberman Lab Podcast, "Mental Health Toolkit: Tools to Bolster Your Mood & Mental Health," October 29, 2023, https://www.hubermanlab.com/episode/mental-health-toolkit-tools-to-bolster-your-mood-mental-health.

16 Gretchen Rubin, "What you do every day matters more than what you do once in a while," November 7, 2011, https://gretchenrubin.com/articles/what-you-do-every-day-matters-more-than-what-you-do-once-in-a-while/

17 E.g., American Psychological Association, "Working out boosts brain health," March 4, 2020, https://www.apa.org/topics/exercise-fitness/stress; Kaiser Permanente, "Regular Exercise Benefits Both Mind and Body: A Psychiatrist Explains," December 22, 2021, https://mydoctor.kaiserpermanente.org/mas/news/regular-exercise-benefits-both-mind-and-body-a-psychiatrist-explains-1903986.

18 James Clear, *Atomic Habits* (New York: Avery, 2018) 16-17.

19 ibid., 162-63.

20 Sarah Wilson, *This One Wild and Precious Life* (Dey St., 2020), 288.

21 ibid., 156.

22 ibid., 156.

23 Renée Onque, CNBC, "Harvard professor who teaches a class on happiness: The happiest people balance and prioritize 3 things," April 20, 2024, https://www.cnbc.com/2024/04/20/arthur-c-brooks-the-3-macronutrients-of-happiness.html.

24 ibid.

25 Bill Perkins, *Die with Zero: Getting All You Can from Your Money and Your Life* (New York: Houghton Mifflin Harcourt, 2020), 52-53.

26 ibid., 43-35.

27 Greg McKeown, *Essentialism: The Disciplined Pursuit of Less* (United Kingdom: Virgin Books, 2014), 5.

28 Jake Knapp & John Zeratsky, *Make Time: How to Focus on What Matters Every Day* (New York: Currency, 2018), 4-5.

29 ibid., 6.

30 Elizabeth Gilbert, *Big Magic: Creative Living Beyond Fear* (New York: Riverhead Books, 2015), 8.

31 ibid.

32 U.S. Bureau of Labor Statistics, Occupational Employment and Wages, May 2023, 23-1011 Lawyers, https://www.bls.gov/oes/current/oes231011.htm.

33 ibid.

34 https://www.gallup.com/cliftonstrengths/en/252137/home.aspx.

35 Although taking classes for fun is great too if you're only doing it for the experience without attaching some lofty, unreasonable expectation of grand success.

36 Sarah Cottrell, The Former Lawyer Podcast, https://formerlawyer.com/category/podcast/page/26/.

37 *Atomic Habits*, 16-17.

38 ibid., 17-18.

39 Cal Newport, *Slow Productivity: The Lost Art of Accomplishment Without Burnout* (Portfolio/Penguin, 2024), 147.

40 Merriam-Webster Dictionary, https://www.merriam-webster.com/dictionary/boundary.

41 Shawn Askinosie, *Meaningful Work: A Quest to Do Great Business, Find Your Calling, and Feed Your Soul* (TarcherPerigee Books, 2017), 8-9.

42 ibid., 13-14.

43 ibid., 19-20.

44 Leo Tolstoy, *Anna Karenina*, (C. Garnett, Trans., International Collectors Library, 1944), 1.

Printed in the United States
by Baker & Taylor Publisher Services